BOUND *to* LOSE

DESTINED *to* WIN

Dan Mac

Received 12/20/16

ISBN: 1-4610-4781-1
ISBN-13: 9781461047810

Contents

DEDICATION AND THANKS

This book is dedicated to my mother, Evangelist Erma Jean Kelley, you and your prayers brought me through one evil adventure after another. Your prayers brought me through voodoo, drugs, gangs and an abortion attempt. You fought with all your might to keep me alive. Your faith in God sets my mind on this scripture found in Romans 12:3; According as God has dealt to every man the measure of faith. You were given great faith by God and you used it. I love you Mom

To my wife Selena Edwards-Kelley of 30 years, you were either sent by God or you were out of your mind to marry a man like me. Our backgrounds are so different. You are a loving woman, a woman of honor, integrity and faithful to our Lord and Savior Jesus Christ. I love you wife.

To my mother and father-in-law, thank you so much for all your love and kindness throughout the years. I love and appreciate you.

To my sister Evangelist Chandler Jean "Sissy" Kelley-Miller, who stayed in my face telling me about being saved until you got me to that church. Thanks for being so bold for Jesus. Because of you not only did I get saved and filled with the Holy Ghost, now many souls are getting saved through my testimony.

To all my brothers and sisters, Robert (Bobby), Chandler, Rickey, Phyllis, Jacqueline, Cora, Allean and Terence, I thank you and I love you.

To all of my children, Curtis II, Keme, Scott, Zina, Angelia, Christopher and Cherish, I love you all. To my grandchildren and soon to be great grandchild, Papa loves you.

To my church family The Bridge of Deliverance Church, I love you.

To Paul and Jan Crouch, thanks for allowing me to be a part of the TBN family. I love and appreciate you both.

To Benny Hinn, for those powerful words you spoke to me. To Rod Parsley, for laying hands on me and praying for me. To Apostle Joe Lee Hughes and Lucy B. Hughes, thanks for the training. To Pastors Tony and Cynthia Brazelton, thanks for you love, encouragement and support. I love you all.

I will love you, O LORD, my strength.
The LORD is my rock and my fortress and my deliverer;
My God, my strength, in whom I will trust;
My shield and the horn of my salvation, my stronghold.
I will call upon the LORD, who is worthy to be praised;
So shall I be saved from my enemies.

The pangs of death surrounded me,
And the floods of ungodliness made me afraid.
The sorrows of Sheol surrounded me;
The snares of death confronted me.
In my distress I called upon the LORD,
And cried out to my God;
He heard my voice from His temple,
And my cry came before Him, even to His ears.

Psalm 18:1-6

Preface

"We do not look at the things which are seen, but at the things which are not seen. For the things which are seen are temporary, but the things which are not seen are eternal."

- 2 Corinthians 4:18

Throughout the Bible we read about miracles, supernatural events, and the visible and invisible realm. From a young age, even though I had little knowledge of the Bible, I understood that the invisible realm is just as real—and sometimes more real—than the visible realm that we see and live in every day.

I think about the story in 2 Kings 6:8-18 when the king of Syria went to war against the children of Israel. When a servant of Elisha expressed fear that the children of Israel would not have the manpower to fight the Syrians, Elisha told them, "Do not fear, for those who are with us are more than those who are with them." Elisha prayed, "Lord, open his eyes that he may see."

When the Lord opened the young man's eyes, he saw a mountain full of horses and chariots of fire all around Elisha. God let this young man see into the invisible realm and view the warriors that God had sent to fight the battle for the children of Israel.

There are similar stories throughout the Bible. Still today, God sometimes allows people to see a visible manifestation of the invisible realm so they can understand what is happening "behind the scenes." Sometimes we see angels and the fighting forces sent by God; other times we see into the demonic realm. I was one of those whom God allowed to see into the invisible realm.

My story takes you "behind the scenes," where the invisible realm becomes visible. My father was training me in the occult from the age of five, and the enemy and his forces of darkness tried to ruin my life and kill me many times. But God was there all along, protecting me with His army of angels until I finally accepted Christ and turned my life over to Him. God took everything that the enemy meant for evil and turned it into a testimony to be used for His glory. You will find that the things of God, even those things in the invisible realm, are very real and much more powerful than any spirit from the kingdom of hell.

My testimony is also a story of deliverance. I am a deliverance minister, and I hope that this book will serve as a manual for those who want to be used by God to help deliver people from the bondages of sin in which Satan has them bound. I believe it will also help you live your own life in the victory that Jesus purchased for you at the cross.

After having received years of training in the occult, I know much about the demonic realm. I also was trained to know the names of the demonic spirits with which I am dealing. When I minister to people one-on-one, I explain to them what spirit they are dealing with, and I pray by casting out that particular spirit. I do not ask the spirit to identify itself; I simply know the name of the spirit by the manifestation of that spirit in the person's life.

I questioned whether or not to identify by name some of the spirits that I discussed in this book. The manuscript was written with that information included, and then revised with the information removed. We found that the book was more effective with that information left in. This will be controversial in some Christian circles, but as you read this book, you will learn the identity of some of these spirits. I believe that knowing their identity exposes more of the enemy and shines the light of Jesus into the enemy's realm of darkness.

If you are involved in deliverance ministry, this information will help you know exactly what you are dealing with. If you are spiritually mature and living a righteous life, please use wisdom and allow the Holy Spirit to lead you in deliverance. Pray, fast, study the Bible, know what you are doing, and make sure your life is holy before the Lord. Some evil spirits come out only through prayer and fasting. People have made mistakes in the past by attempting to cast out evil spirits that they were not prepared to handle. Again, please use wisdom and be led by the Holy Spirit. Do not operate in a fleshly realm and cause problems for yourself and others.

That being said, I want to give this warning. If you are not a Believer who is serving the Lord Jesus Christ, and if you are not living a holy and righteous life before God, you have absolutely no authority to cast out evil spirits. If you have accepted Christ but are living with unrepentant sin, you have no authority to cast out evil spirits. Without spiritual authority, if you attempt to cast out demonic spirits, you might find yourself in the same position as the seven sons of Sceva—overpowered, wounded, and stripped naked by spirits you had no authority to handle.

May the Lord richly bless you as you turn the page and enter the world that I lived in, beginning as a young child. My prayer is that, by the time you finish reading this book, your life will be transformed by the power of the Holy Spirit, and that you will close all the doors you have opened that have allowed the enemy access into your life. I pray that this book will teach you how to keep the enemy under your feet and live the kind of victorious life that Jesus promised. Live so that you receive all of the blessings Jesus promised, in both this life and the one hereafter!

CHAPTER 1

Life with a Wicked Man

"A wise man fears and departs from evil, but a fool rages and is self-confident. A quick-tempered man acts foolishly, and a man of wicked intentions is hated."
- Proverbs 14:16-17

"Erma, stay away from that guy. He's bad. There's something about that man that's not right."

"But everybody else is married. I want to get married, too! I don't want to be an old maid." Besides, he was such a handsome young man. And that is why Erma Jean McCulley, a Spirit-filled believer who attended a Church of God in Christ, married Robert Kelley, the man that her uncle and pastor warned her to stay away from.

Robert met Erma in Vallejo, California in the hospital where they both worked. She was a nursing student; he was a janitor. Nursing students were not permitted to have conversations with the employees, but Robert kept his eye on Erma. He cornered her one day to tell her he'd been watching her. In the beginning she ignored his increasingly flirtatious advances, but he was not a man who gave up easily. He learned where she attended church and showed up for services.

As it turned out, Robert was a hypocrite who had no problem pretending that he and Jesus were best buddies who went back a long way. That pretense, along with his looks, smooth talk, and shower of attention, sucked Erma into a cruel vacuum from which she would not escape until Robert died twenty-six years later. From the time they married in

1947, he made life miserable for Erma and their ten living children, of whom I was one.

A father should be the protector and spiritual leader of his family. He is called to submit to God as the head of his household, loving his wife as Christ loves the church. As a man under submission, a father should obey God. He should be the priest of the household, instructing his family in righteousness and setting an upright example for them to follow.

Our dad was a priest all right—a voodoo priest. And instead of loving his wife as Christ loves the church, he was a man with an iron fist who often beat her to the ground. Instead of a protector of his family, he was an abusive man whose explosive rage and ungodly behavior loosed demons from hell into our home. He is no longer alive, but the effect of his actions lives on.

Parents should give their children the gift of a godly heritage. I am thankful that, through all the torment, my mother had the strength to hold fast to her faith in God, to anoint her children with oil and pray blessings and protection over us, and to teach us the ways of righteousness, even though my father fought her every way imaginable.

Robert Kelley had a generational history of voodoo, but my mother did not know that before she married him. None of us knew the full story until we traced our family lineage through genealogical archives kept by the Mormon Church in Salt Lake City, Utah.

Through research, we learned about a potato farmer in Ireland named John Kelley. In 1846 the potato crop in Ireland failed, and terrible famine and disease followed. John Kelley decided he could no longer deal with it, so he packed his family and belongings and moved to Hispaniola. Today that island is split between Haiti and the Dominican Republic.

There John Kelley started a plantation with about forty slaves, all of whom were already on the island when he arrived. The slave trade was flourishing at that time, and all of Kelley's slaves had arrived in Hispaniola from Africa.

Dad's sisters, who are now deceased, talked about the slave master, John Kelley. My aunts took most their information to the grave with them, but we did hear stories about the curses. Since most Africans practiced voodoo and other forms of witchcraft, they brought their religion to the islands and remained attached to it. Often they integrated their voodoo practices into Roman Catholicism. John Kelley's African slaves placed voodoo curses on him by sending a hot wind to burn his crops. His wife also became ill.

When Kelley realized his business was failing, he gathered his belongings, including some slaves, and moved to New Orleans. A few slaves escaped into the bush before Kelley could get them onto the ship, but he still brought ten slaves to America.

Two of the ten slaves were Pinky and her brother, Cupid. Since the slaves were still practicing voodoo, once again they cursed Kelley after he arrived in New Orleans. By this time Kelley had become a frail old man and his slaves were escaping into the swamps of New Orleans. So John Kelley moved west to Texas and took Cupid with him. Eventually Cupid fathered a son that he named Cupid, Jr., who would one day become my grandfather.

Since slaves were given the last name of their slave owner, my ancestors became known as Kelley's. Cupid Kelley, Jr. fathered a son named Robert who was born in Texas in 1917. As a young man, Robert left Texas and moved to California. Erma Jean McCulley was born July 4, 1926, and she left Memphis, Tennessee and moved to California to further her education. That is where she and Robert met.

Two of Dad's relatives became Jehovah's Witnesses, his sister Catherine was a devout Christian, and his mother became a Baptist, mostly in name only. Dad pretended to be a Baptist, but I'll tell you more of that story later in the book. Dad had eight sisters and one brother. I never met his brother who died years ago in San Francisco. Nobody in the Kelley family ever broke the generational curse of voodoo. It followed them from Africa to Haiti, then from New Orleans to Texas, then to Vallejo, California, and finally to Stamford, Connecticut where Robert and Erma moved in 1951. I was born and raised in the projects of Stamford, Connecticut.

One of my earliest memories is of a dream I had at age three. In this dream, I was in the kitchen looking out the window at a playmate of mine standing outside. Suddenly the ground began to shake, and I yelled for her to come inside. She didn't seem to hear me. Then the earth opened up and she fell inside. The earth closed around her as the ground kept shaking. I heard a voice say, "Because of you, the ground is shaking. Because of you, the ground is broken."

I woke up sobbing. When morning arrived, I learned that my friend was okay. The following night I had the very same dream.

I never told anybody that dream, not even my mother. For years that dream caused me to blame myself for every bad thing that happened. As a child I had no idea what the dream meant. Today I hope it means that, instead of people being swallowed up by demonic forces, God will use me to bring deliverance and to help people become consumed by Him. It is interesting that years later, during my boxing career, I was given the nickname Earthquake.

Stamford, Connecticut borders Long Island Sound, and we could look outside our front door and see the top half of the Empire State Building in New York Harbor. When somebody committed a crime in New York City, they often hid in Stamford. In those days, during the 1950s and 1960s, police would shoot to kill and ask questions later. Out of anger at the police, people sometimes harbored these criminals. Our family harbored a few of them, too. The police must have known about it, because I recall the FBI visiting our home to look for a man who was not there.

Our home at 69 Putnam Lane in South Field Village was half Christian and half bondage. My mother was a godly woman who always prayed, blessed her children, and emphasized the Word of God. She always taught us about the goodness of God and His Holy Spirit.

Then there was Dad. He was funny at times, and evil or weird at other times. He liked to travel, study science, and dress well. He owned a painting business because he thought that if you knew how to paint houses, you would never be broke. He chased women and believed that if you didn't have a woman at all times, you were either a sissy or a homosexual. I never saw him steal, but I saw him do just about everything else. He drank liquor, with Thunderbird and Old Crow Whiskey being his favorites. When he got drunk, it seemed that somebody else had crawled inside his body. He wasn't evil every moment of his life, but the bad moments far outweighed the good. One of the few pleasant memories I have of him is when he took us to an amusement park and carried me on his shoulders.

I had nine living brothers and sisters: Bobby, Richard, Chandler, Elvin, Jacqueline, Phyllis, Cora, Alleyne, and Terence. Christopher, the last child, was stillborn. I was child number seven. After I became an adult, my mother told me the story of how my father tried to kill me before I was born.

Dad didn't want another child, and when he learned that my mother was pregnant, he demanded that she have an abortion. She refused. He tried unsuccessfully to kill me by kicking and beating her in the stomach. That didn't work, so he dragged her down a flight of stairs and took her to have an abortion. In those days abortion was illegal, but Dad knew a doctor who performed abortions on the students at Yale. My mother said that, as the doctor tried to perform the abortion, she felt an invisible hand protecting me. The abortion failed and, miraculously, I was born perfectly normal.

When the witches in Brooklyn learned that Dad tried to have me aborted, they were furious. "You can't sacrifice your seventh child!" they told him. "Don't you know the seventh child is chosen?"

At the age of eleven I would learn what it meant to be chosen. But I had a few other things to learn first. Unfortunately, it didn't take long for me to discover the world of drugs.

By the time I was four years old, two of my older brothers, ages ten and thirteen, were selling drugs. They got the drugs from somebody in New York City, and the Kelleys became the first drug dealers in our neighborhood. They sold just about anything a drug user wanted, including cocaine, valium, quaaludes, heroin, amphetamines, and LSD. People from all walks of life came to our house to buy drugs. People you wouldn't dream of being on drugs were buying drugs. The drug users soon developed an addiction and a desire for harder, more effective drugs which my brothers were eager to supply. Both of my brothers spent many years in jail for dealing drugs.

Along with selling, my brothers were drug users. They didn't mind using their drugs around Dad, but they would never use them around Mom. She was a Holy Spirit-filled woman who attended a Church of God in Christ, and she was from the school that said you don't play Checkers, much less do drugs.

I watched as my brothers rolled and smoked marijuana. I watched as they tied a belt around their arms and shot a needle of heroin into a budging vein. I watched them smoke, shoot, and snort until it appeared that their body was here but their mind was somewhere else. They seemed to be in another universe.

They were my older brothers, so of course I wanted to copy everything they did. I wanted to go to their universe, even though that world could quickly become the hell of no return. Drugs led to abuse, violence, arrest, job loss, family breakup, health problems, and death. But what did any of that mean to a four-year-old?

"I want to do that, too," I told my brothers. "I want to shoot that stuff in my arms."

"No, you can't. You're too young," they replied.

"I'm not too young. I can do it."

"No! You're too young."

Their response to my persistent pleas was always the same: No, you're too young. Each time they told me no, I went to my bedroom to pout. Then one day I felt a presence in my room that gave me a creepy feeling, as though an evil person that I could not see was in the room with me. Instead of the name Curtis, I was often called Kurt, Kirk, and sometimes Kirkie. As I sat in my room, I heard a voice call, "Kirk, you don't have to be sad because they won't give you their drugs. You can get high, too. You don't have to ask them for anything. I'll show you how to get high. Take some of your plastic toys and go to the kitchen."

I gathered some plastic toys and went to the kitchen.

The voice instructed, "Turn on the stove."

"I can't reach it," I replied.

"Get a chair."

Still I could not see anybody. But I clearly heard a voice and knew that an invisible presence was with me. I obeyed and got a chair. The voice gave specific instructions, telling me where to put the chair and how to turn on the stove burner. Then the voice said, "Now hold your toys over the burner and inhale the fumes." Again I obeyed.

"Let the smoke go up your nose. Inhale all the smoke. The more you inhale, the higher you'll get."

That might sound bizarre; but folks, let me tell you something. When people say they heard voices telling them to do evil things, believe it. They absolutely are hearing voices—the voices of demons from hell. A demonic spirit was speaking to me and instructing me in evil at the tender age of four.

When I saw that I could get high by inhaling fumes from my plastic toys, I burned more of them to get high. Each time, the voice of an invisible, hellish demon was there to give me detailed instructions. I got so high that I was often in another realm for hours at a time. It seemed that each time I got high, another door opened and I entered that room and stay there for hours. When the high left, I suffered shakes and other withdrawal symptoms.

Before long I had melted most of my plastic toys. But I learned that almost anything in your home can be turned into a drug. The voice of this same demonic spirit instructed me to burn other household items and inhale them. As I obeyed, this voice was at my side giving me step-by-step instructions.

Even at that age, the enemy was trying to destroy my life with inhalants. The intended side effects of these inhalants are loss of inhibitions and a sense of euphoria and excitement. The unintended side effects are dizziness, amnesia, inability to concentrate, mental confusion, impaired judgment, and hallucinations. But I would soon learn that some of the things you see are not hallucinations; they are very real.

One day I decided to burn a whole bag of plastic soldiers. They burned quickly, and things got out of control as smoke filled the kitchen and the molten plastic dripped onto the floor. Still, the voice kept telling me, "Burn some more! Burn more! Keep burning them!"

A large drop of melted plastic dripped onto my thumb, burning through my flesh and down to the bone. The pain was intense. When I tried to pull the plastic off my thumb, skin came off with it. I wanted to stop burning the soldiers, but I had lost control of the situation. Somebody was shaking my chair, and I even heard laughter as the voice mocked me when I burned myself and nearly fell off the chair.

Meanwhile, the voice was still saying, "Don't stop! Keep burning the soldiers!"

I shouted, "No, I'm stopping! I'm not doing this anymore!" When this invisible being knew that I meant business, the spirit materialized before my eyes. I actually saw the outline of an ugly creature with a smirk on its face. This creature put its arm around me and insisted, "No, you can't stop."

That incident frightened me so badly that I stopped burning toys and didn't try to get high for the next two years. But I still could not get away from that evil spirit that wanted to destroy my life with drugs. The force was gaining strength on me every day. Eventually it won. At the age of six, I was smoking marijuana. At age ten I was using cocaine. And by age twelve, I had a five hundred dollar a day cocaine habit. I also bought a chemistry set and made my own drugs.

Even before I had a chance to experiment with other drugs, my life went from bad to worse. No sooner had I stopped burning toys than another demonic voice stepped in. This time it was the deep, bellowing voice of a six foot two inch man of iron; it was the voice of the man I called Dad.

When I was five years old, he decided that I should run numbers for him. Running numbers is part of illegal gambling and, for the next several years, I ran his numbers. In our neighborhood was a man who operated a betting house for people in New York City. The mobsters and gamblers in New York City wouldn't dare come into the Stamford projects, but they paid bookies in the projects to oversee the gambling business for them.

People gambled on different things—horses, for example. They gambled on which horse would win, and they gambled on what position the horse would hold when it crossed the finish line. My father sent me through the neighborhood to collect numbers and money; then I took the betting numbers and the money to Smitty, the bookie. Dad always told me, "Run the money to Smitty's and don't let your shirttail catch up with you." I didn't know what he meant by that, so I often looked back as I ran to make certain my shirttail wasn't touching my back. I had to run fast to keep the tail of my shirt away from my body.

One woman in the neighborhood gambled based on superstition. If she had the same physical ailment three times that week, she played the number three. She might say, "Kirkie, my bunion hurt me three times this week. I want you to play me the numbers three, three, three. Now you run down there as fast as you can and play this for me. And by the way, here's some extra money. You bring me back some of that chewing tobacco."

I had to remember every house, every bet, and every dollar. We were not supposed to write anything down because if we were caught, we had to be sure there was no written record. Dad forced me to run the numbers because he knew the police would never suspect a five-year old. Indeed, never once did the police stop me.

When I ran the numbers and the money to the bookie's house, they always seemed to know I was coming. Smitty addressed me like an adult as he said, "Okay, I'll be right with you." Five guys answered the phones, while others counted money and pulled the crank on a machine. The men had tiny, thin strips of paper with the numbers written on them. These were pieces of paper that could easily be destroyed if the place was raided. And on one particular day, I arrived just before Smitty's was raided.

Before I could finish my business with the bookie, the police burst through the door. I still had the money in my pocket at the time. The police had clubs, so I was sure they were going to beat me with their clubs. Without being touched, I could almost feel the clubs bashing me on the head.

But when the policemen saw me, one of them came to me and said, "What are you doing here, you snotty-nosed little brat? This is no place for a kid. You need to get out of here." He led me to the door and said, "Now go outside and play."

Once outside, I rushed home as quickly as my legs would carry me. I bolted through the door and saw Dad sitting at the dinner table. "The police are at Smitty's!" I exclaimed.

In his booming voice that reminded me of a foghorn, he replied, "I heard about it." He held out his hand. "Where's the money? Give me the money."

He didn't ask if I was okay; he was concerned only about the money. That wasn't a surprise since Dad was abusive to every person in the family. He was a selfish and evil man whose wrath was felt by each of us. But there was no question he hated me. I recall the first time he hit me. I was a young child playing in the yard with the neighborhood children when Dad called for me, but I didn't hear him. Since I didn't answer, he bolted into the yard and hit me on the head with a mallet.

From that day forward, he beat me regularly. Each time I did something that he thought was wrong, he punished me by removing his belt and repeatedly swinging it and hitting me in the head with the belt buckle while threatening to kill me. He forced me to stand in the corner for hours with a bloody head. If I cried, he beat me. If I moved, he beat me. He wouldn't let me or anybody in the family wipe the blood off my head. If my mother came to my aid, he beat her, too. Other times he made me eat table scraps from the garbage can.

One time he threw a chrome kitchen chair at me. The chair didn't hit me, but I felt wind come across my face as the chair flew past me. He didn't need an excuse to beat any of us; the entire family was fearful to even sit at the table and have dinner with him. If he merely suspected someone of being disobedient to his orders, he beat them severely.

For years, every word this man spoke sent fear down my spine. Even as I heard the engine of his Dodge as he drove down the street toward home, I looked for a place to hide. I never wanted to be in the same room with him. I was often sick to my stomach and was diagnosed with ulcers in seventh grade. I was even diagnosed with heart disease. The doctor told my mother that I would not live past ninth grade. The stress of living with my father was almost more than I could handle.

Since he was already a brutal and evil man, it should have been no surprise when Dad brought a Haitian voodoo priestess—I'll call her a witch—into our home to teach me voodoo. I was five years old when she came to live with us.

When this witch moved in, she brought her belongings into the bedroom that I shared with my younger brother. She spread her voodoo paraphernalia across the dresser. I knew something was wrong with this woman because our mother, being a Holy Spirit-filled, Pentecostal woman, had taught us what the Bible says. She taught us about the Holy Spirit. So even at the age of five, I recognized something about this woman that was different from what our mother taught us.

Everything this witch did was dark, evil, and demonic. She had every kind of occult item that you can imagine, and she practiced obeah, santeria, voodoo, and other forms of witchcraft. She even had a doll that talked to her. Many people would never believe this, but I watched it with my own eyes. This was a store-bought doll; but by the time she had it for a while, so many demonic spirits had attached themselves to the doll that it became evil and demonic-looking. No longer did it have the appearance of a cute, store-bought doll. It wasn't the doll itself that talked to the woman, of course, but it was the demonic spirits that had attached themselves to the doll. She kept this doll on the dresser and had conversations with it as demonic spirits gave her instructions. I would not have believed it could happen had I not seen it with my own eyes.

For the next six years, this woman taught me as much as she possibly could about voodoo. Dad—the man who should have been teaching me the righteous things of God—assisted her. Every evening, either he or the witch taught me some aspect of voodoo.

Some of the things Dad taught were so deep and mystical that they meant nothing to me. I sometimes fell asleep as he talked. When I nodded off, he hit me on the head and hollered, "Wake up! Wake up!" I never understood why I had to be the person to learn all of this. Why was he not teaching my older brothers?

The witch pretended to be a devout Christian as she conducted phony church services in our home. She used familiar spirits to tell people things about themselves. People came to our home to hear her speak, and she would point to someone and say "I have a prophecy for you." Instead of prophesying, she told them things they already knew; for example, she would describe items they had in their homes. This witch even took up an offering for herself. Some of the people were convinced that she was the real deal.

You can imagine how all of this upset my mother. "I don't want all of this foolishness going on in my house!" she declared to my father.

"I'm the man of the house and I say what goes on in here!" was his reply. He beat my mother to the ground to keep her under his control.

Having so much demonic activity in our home caused evil spirits to manifest before my eyes. The witch did not sleep in my room at night, but she left all of her paraphernalia on the dresser. Demonic spirits attach themselves to items that are used for occult purposes, so even though this witch was not in my bedroom at night, the room still came alive with demonic sprits.

Grotesque and deformed creatures shook my bed, appeared in my closet, and came out from underneath my bed. One time something crawled from under my bed and it had Dad's face. It even wore the same square glasses. My first thought was, "What is Dad doing under my bed?" But after it crawled out, I saw that the rest of its body was green and covered with fish scales. It moved with a swimming motion as it dived into the floor. I saw such horrible and evil-looking creatures in my room at night that, even as a child, I was a nervous wreck. Sometimes I thought I was going crazy.

I was not the only person in the family who saw these spirits at night. My mother often saw a spirit coming from her bedroom closet that had the appearance of a goat. It frightened her so badly that she sometimes slept on the couch. But the spirits that I saw kept me awake every single night. I feared being in my bedroom, so I often roamed the house. One spirit, which through my voodoo training I learned was called a waster spirit, sometimes chased me through the house at night.

Dad grew angry with me for running through the house while everybody else was in bed. It didn't matter to him that I was being chased and tormented the whole night by evil spirits that he allowed into our home. One night, in a fit of rage, Dad waited for me at the top of the stairs.

When I ran up the stairs, Dad jumped out at me. I said, "Daddy, that thing is chasing me! It's right there at the bottom of the stairs!"

Instead of defending me, he took off his belt and beat me in the head with the belt buckle. He hit me so hard that he cracked my skull. I felt my spirit leave my body, and I hovered above my body and watched as Dad continued to beat me with his belt buckle. I still have a scar on my forehead from that brutal beating.

Meanwhile, the evil spirit that had been chasing me was at the bottom of the stairs laughing. I felt my own spirit come back into my body, and somehow I managed to crawl to my bedroom. Still I could not get away from that evil spirit; it came into my room and taunted me from the closet.

Evil spirits tormented me all night, every night. When I finally fell asleep, I had nightmares. Sometimes I dreamed of being chased by evil spirits, or of falling off a building. Repeatedly I had a dream in which two of my brothers and I were playing tag. A wall with a door came into view, and my brothers were able to run through the door. When I tried to run through it, the door disappeared. With each nightmare, I woke with my heart pounding. Then I looked at the closet and saw the same evil spirit from my dream laughing at me.

For eleven years straight, I was so tormented by these spirits that I slept no more than two hours a night. You can imagine what two hours of sleep a night for eleven years will do to a person. I did not have a good night's rest until I gave my life to Christ.

My dad was the person to thank for all of that torment. He was one of the most powerful voodoo priests on the eastern seaboard; and like the witch, he practiced voodoo, obeah, and other forms of witchcraft. Dad was so deeply involved in the occult that he didn't associate with people who merely dabbled in witchcraft. He associated with people who were so demon possessed that they could come into our home by walking through walls and never opening our front door.

Having no power to make decisions in the home meant that my mother could do nothing to stop my father from engaging in occult activities. He ruled the house with a belt and an iron fist. When my mother was pregnant with her last child, Dad became angry with her and told her, "You're going to be the first woman on the moon and I'm going to send you there!"

He grabbed one of our chrome kitchen chairs and chased her as she ran for her life. While he was chasing her, Dad experienced an asthma attack and was forced to stop running. Mom hid in the closet until he calmed down. The child she was carrying, a boy that she named Christopher, was stillborn.

Dad was a womanizer who often brought other women into our home. One of the women he seemed to love was the Haitian voodoo priestess who lived with us. She was his woman—one of them, at least. One time the witch brought a woman from another country into our home, and my mother had to give up her bedroom for them.

It was not unusual for my mother to hear another woman brag, "Your husband is going out with me tonight." We knew that Dad had a girl-friend and a son in White Plains, New York because the girl showed up at our door one day asking for money. He fathered three more children by a woman in Port Chester. And those are just the ones we knew about.

This is a good place to mention that my father—as unbelievable as this might seem—was a Baptist preacher. While my mother attended a Church of God in Christ, Dad occasionally attended a Baptist church. Dad was an intelligent man who knew exactly what the Bible said;

he read it from cover to cover seven times. God had never called him to preach, but he preached anyway. And what a preacher he was. The church he attended had preaching contests and Dad always won the prize: a ham and a turkey.

He had everybody in the church fooled; but one day his sins found him out. Dad was at a bar in Port Chester, New York with one of his girlfriends. She did something that angered him, and he beat her up. When the police arrived, his glasses were broken and his face was bloody. He was hauled to jail on Thursday and released the following Tuesday.

When Dad appeared in court, the judge discovered that he was married and had lied about it. When the judge learned that Dad gave his girlfriend eighty-seven dollars a week and his wife fifteen dollars a week, he was furious. He sentenced Dad to six months in jail.

The incident was reported in the newspaper, and the story proved embarrassing for the Baptist church Dad attended. The jig was up. They kicked him out of the church and he never preached again. That was the end of our free hams and turkeys.

Through all of this, my mother miraculously kept the faith and always prayed over each of her children. While Dad spoke curses over us in the Creole language, Mom spoke blessings over us. When Dad told me that I had an obligation to carry on his voodoo legacy, Mom prayed. She often told me that I would grow up to be a man of God who would preach the Gospel.

My mother was filled with the Holy Spirit, and she had two weapons. One of them was prayer. She always anointed our heads with oil as she prayed for us. Her other weapon was the baptism of the Holy Spirit. She often sat in her rocking chair and prayed for us in her heavenly prayer language. It would have been easy for her to give up because, when Dad caught her praying for us, he beat her.

Surely it must have seemed that her prayers would never be answered. We had all kinds of sin in our family; we had thieves, witches, drug dealers, drug addicts, and a Black Panthers activist. Yet no matter how hopeless things looked, our mother ignored the circumstances and kept praying for us. And she didn't mind telling people who tried to harm one of her children that they had better keep their hands off her child. I have never stopped thanking God for a praying mother.

CHAPTER 2

A Curse of Voodoo

"There shall not be found among you anyone who...practices witchcraft, or a
soothsayer, or one who interprets omens, or a sorcerer, or one who conjures spells,
or a medium, or a spiritist, or one who calls up the dead."
- Deuteronomy 18:10-11

Despite my mother's prayers, I plunged deeper into sin. There was something about voodoo that intrigued me. I despised being tormented by demonic spirits, but I was drawn to the power behind the occult. Witches and voodoo practitioners are deceived into thinking they are doing good things for people; but in reality, they are simply controlling people. I learned that I could control my life, control other people, and get what I wanted without waiting for it. People who are self-centered, greedy, or looking for a quick fix to their problems in life find the occult appealing. Darkness is selfish; it wants everything right now. That described me. I wanted my stuff now—my money, my power, and my respect.

You cannot be taught voodoo without learning to curse people and cast spells on them. I had seen my grandmother cast a spell when I was five years old. She and a man were in a heated argument, and I heard her speak some strange words to him. When the words left her mouth, the man fell over backwards and appeared to be dead. That shocked me, but I was impressed enough to wonder what might happen if I spoke those same words. I gathered enough courage to utter the words she spoke. When I did, I felt as though something entered my body and wouldn't leave. I believe that, even as a child, I spoke words that allowed a demonic spirit to attack me. Words are powerful, even when spoken by children.

Once I learned to cast spells and speak curses, I exercised that power over anybody who crossed me the wrong way. On one occasion, a man in the neighborhood was harassing me and my friends. We told the man to stop, but he continued. My friends pointed to me and warned him, "Do you know what this guy can do to you?" Still he persisted.

I looked at the man and said, "Okay, you asked for it. Within twenty-four hours, you will be dead." The next afternoon somebody shot the man dead.

One thing I learned was that I could not cast a spell on a born-again Christian. I also learned who was more powerful than the spirits I served.

There were two boys, the Davis brothers, who attended my school. We played basketball together and got along well most of the time. Their mother and my mother were friends. But one day the Davis brothers got saved. They abandoned us by turning to Jesus, and suddenly I didn't like those boys anymore. Another reason I didn't like them was because they were causing us to lose drug customers, and I didn't appreciate losing customers to Jesus. So I decided to use my voodoo training to curse them.

I sent an evil sprit to harm the Davis brothers. But the spirit came back and said, "I can't touch those boys."

I sent it back to try again. Once more it returned and said, "I can't touch them."

By time I was so deeply involved in the occult that I practiced astral projection, or what is sometimes called soul travel. That is the demonic practice whereby a person forces their spirit to leave their body so it can travel to another location. I decided to go there in the spirit realm and see for myself why this evil spirit couldn't touch the Davis brothers.

When I arrived, I was shocked to see two eight-foot tall angels with flaming swords surrounding those boys and guarding them like warriors. They turned from side to side with their swords extended, as though they were ready for battle. I thought to myself, "How can these things be stronger than I am?"

From then on, I made sure I was nice to the Davis brothers. But the tragic part of the story is that those boys turned their backs on God. When I saw them in a nightclub drinking and dancing, I was angry with them. I was not even saved at the time; I was just a wretched sinner who was wrapped up in the occult. But I wanted to shake those boys and say, "Are you crazy? Do you have any idea who was protecting you? I didn't have anything that could touch those angels. And now you turn your back on God!"

That is why it pays to be saved, obedient, and filled with the Holy Spirit. There is no greater protection. There is not an evil person or a demon in hell that can curse you or put a spell on you when you are protected by God and His eight-foot angels with flaming swords. You might not see them in the visible realm, but the protection is there.

I am reminded of a lesson my seventh grade science teacher taught us. In class one day, he told us that there are many things in our water that are invisible to the naked eye. Since I knew more than the teacher, I responded, "No way. There's nothing in water. It's clear. How can there be anything in water?"

He replied, "Okay. You think you know everything. Get some water out of the faucet."

I did, and we put some water between two glass slides. We slipped the slides under the microscope.

"Now, look in the microscope and tell me what you see."

When I looked, I could hardly believe my eyes. There were all kinds of squiggly things moving around and jumping in the water. "Oh, man! You mean all those things are in one little drop of water?"

The teacher told us something that has stayed with me to this day. He said, "Here's a lesson for you. Just because you can't see something doesn't mean it isn't there."

That same truth applies to the spirit realm. Some Christians are like Curtis, the seventh grader who thought he knew more than his teacher. They might believe heavenly angels exist, but they think the demonic spirit realm does not exist. And since they deny the existence of the demonic realm, then of course they don't believe that demonic spirits are real. If they can't see them, then surely they don't exist.

But take it from one with personal experience: demonic spirits are real. Sometimes the things you *don't* see in the invisible realm are more real than the things you *do* see in the visible realm. Just because you can't see something doesn't mean it isn't there.

In countries like Haiti where voodoo is still practiced, people who are involved in the occult don't use guns and knives to kill people. They order demons in the unseen spirit realm to kill people through curses and spells. That way, when somebody dies, nobody can trace the killer. The objective is to get the job done and stay out of jail. Sometimes the person who was cursed simply drops dead from a sudden, unexplained illness. That is the way my dad was taught, and that is the way I was being taught.

Between my dad and the witch, I was learning things that no child should ever be taught. The first thing I learned was the names and assigned duties of the spirits that attach themselves to people who engage in sexual relationships outside of marriage. I learned about erzulie, the main principality that rules over any kind of sexual perversion. I learned how that some voodoo practitioners pray to this spirit, beat drums, go into a trance, and have sexual relations with people all night long—and sometimes all week long.

I learned about twenty-four hour curses, ten-year curses, and twenty-year curses. I was taught how to slow down a person's business. I learned about pavor nocturnus, the spirit that chokes people to death by using its oversized hands, its wings, or a rope. It even smothers babies while they are in bed and causes sudden infant death syndrome. Haitians call it the spirit with the noose. I learned about the fox spirit that causes separation and division; the highway spirit that causes accidents and deaths on the roads; the run-ahead demon that goes ahead of you to cause problems before you arrive at your destination; and the cloaking spirit that hides things and makes them seem to disappear—anything from your car keys to the Statue of Liberty. I learned about the waster spirit and the big face spirit, both of which tormented me every night for eleven years.

Demonic spirits have levels of authority, and higher level spirits dispatch lower level spirits to perform specific duties. It works like a management hierarchy.

I was taught a thousand different methods of voodoo and the names and duties of the spirits behind the occult. After years of being taught voodoo, sleeping two hours a night, and living with evil spirits and a father who was a maniac, I became mean and full of rage. The neighborhood where we lived made up for any negative influence I might have missed at home. The area was full of drug addicts, alcoholics, thieves, rapists, and murderers. Unmarried women were giving birth to children and men were irresponsible. I saw one man attack another man for having an affair with his wife, and I watched the adulterer beg for mercy as the woman's husband used a knife to cut chunks of flesh from the man's face.

If you lived in the projects of Stamford, you were forced to join a gang for protection. Since any gang member would kill you as easily as look at you, gang membership became your method of survival.

Rival gangs fought each other. When sitting in a restaurant, we learned that we must never turn our backs to the door. We always made sure we took the cap off the salt shaker at the table so that we could throw salt in someone's face if we were attacked. The heel of a shoe could be used as a hammer.

In our neighborhood was a notoriously violent gang called the Connecticut Liberals. These gang members destroyed the lives of many people, and they were infamous for raping girls. They gathered in large groups and prowled the neighborhood, looking for an innocent girl to rape. They referred to their prowls as train raids. I was a young boy when the gang asked me to come along on a train raid. I thought they were planning to rob a train, which sounded like fun, so I went along.

But they were not after a train; they were after a girl. They found one, and I watched twenty gang members rape one girl. Even as a young boy, I could not understand how someone could do that to another human being. If I had been older and had access to a gun, I might have shot all twenty of those gang members.

It is interesting to note that almost every one of those guys died at a young age. Some sat in a chair and simply stopped breathing. Some died in their teens, while others died in their twenties. As I recall, only three from the entire gang did not die prematurely.

In our neighborhood were two rival gangs, and we decided it was stupid for us to fight each other when we had other gangs to worry about. So we called a truce. We held a baseball game between the two gangs as part of our truce. It was my turn to run and I made it to second base. When I did, one of the rival gang members pulled a switchblade and tried to cut my throat. I felt a hand, almost like a rush of wind, as it moved me out of the way. Instead of cutting my throat, he cut me across the face in such a manner that it looked as though I had two mouths. That is another scar that I carry to this day.

Later I tried to set up this guy's death. I knew that he always came to the same spot every day, so I waited for him. But he never showed up at that spot. As I stood waiting for him, I heard a voice say, "Don't do it." I mumbled to myself, "He cut my face. I'm killing him." Then the thought crossed my mind that this must be the voice of God that my mother keeps talking about. I didn't harm that gang member, but for as long as we lived in Stamford, he picked on me and verbally abused me.

I was not a large boy at that time, but I developed a reputation for being a fighter. Boys would jump me in a group but never individually. One time I was attacked by two guys in my neighborhood and I successfully fought both of them. Another guy grabbed me from behind and had his fingers around my neck. I put his hand in my mouth and nearly bit off one of his fingers. After that they were more careful around me. I also started carrying a sharp razor as a weapon.

Back at our home, Dad occasionally invited a group of witches and voodoo practitioners over for a party. They came at night after the rest of us were in bed, and we could hear them in our living room laughing, singing, snapping their fingers to the music, and engaging in all kinds of merriment. For a reason that I never understood, the men always dressed in tight, powder blue suits.

Since I was awake most of the night, sometimes I slipped out of my room and into the living room hoping to observe and perhaps join the festivities. As I eagerly ran down the stairs toward the living room, each time I heard them say, "Here he comes!" I've already mentioned that Dad's friends were so demonic they could walk through walls. They could also disappear in the blink of an eye. When I rounded the corner to the living room, within seconds every person in the room vanished.

Just like the situation with my brothers and their drugs, I found myself on the outside looking in and wanting to be part of something I could not join. Was this a trick of the enemy to entice me with something I could not have?

If that was the plan, it worked. I decided that I would do whatever it took to become a sorcerer. I must have been a very good student because, when I was eleven years old, I learned that I was ready for a promotion.

First, the witch who was teaching me voodoo said, "You are no longer your mother's child. You belong to me. You must start calling me 'mother.'"

"My mom didn't tell me to call you mother," I shot back. I refused to call her anything except Madam, which is what she asked everybody else to call her. I knew that my mother loved all of her children, and she never would have given me to another woman.

Then the witch revealed her true purpose for being in our home. "I was sent here from Haiti to train you. There is a delegation in Haiti that is waiting for you because you are the chosen one."

"What do you mean, chosen?" I asked.

"You have been chosen to work with Papa Doc Duvalier. You are Haitian. You are the seventh child born to your father, so you are special—a chosen one. I have been here to train you. Start packing your clothes because you are going with me to Port-au-Prince."

Years later, after I became a Christian and studied the Bible, I understood the significance of the number seven. To God, the number seven is a holy number that stands for completion and fulfillment. Since the enemy imitates and perverts the things of God, that explains why, as the seventh child of a Haitian voodoo priest, I was chosen to continue the curse and fulfill Satan's purposes in the demonic realm.

I had never heard of Haiti, nor did I know that Francois "Papa Doc" Duvalier had been the villainous dictator of Haiti since 1957. He was a cruel and depraved man who, according to historical records, killed as many as fifty thousand Haitians while he ruled the country. He was also a voodoo priest who used his power to manipulate and control people. Papa Doc died in 1971 at the age of sixty-four and left his equally wicked son in charge. During the years that Papa Doc and his son ruled Haiti, the country became known as the most impoverished in the Western Hemisphere.

I might have known nothing about Haiti and Papa Doc, but to an eleven-year-old boy who had barely been outside of Stamford, Connecticut, the thought of taking a boat trip to a far-away island to become a sorcerer was quite a thrill. I even bragged to Bishop I. L. Jefferson, pastor of the Church of God in Christ and a distant cousin on my mother's side, that I was going to Haiti. "Bishop, I'm going to Haiti. I'm going to be a sorcerer in Haiti!"

"You're not going to Haiti," he replied. "I rebuke that in the name of Jesus. You will not go to Haiti. You're going to be a minister of the Gospel of Jesus Christ." Bishop laid hands on me and prayed. "The devil will not get this boy. He is a child of God, and God is going to save him from witchcraft and voodoo. God will use him mightily. He is going to become a Bishop like me and preach the Gospel around the world."

I wondered how I could be a preacher of the Gospel and practice voodoo at the same time.

Dad and the witch completed the arrangements for my trip, and the witch packed my clothes in an old brown suitcase. Dad came to my room early one morning and said, "You ready to go, boy? I'm putting you on the boat."

He planned to put me and the witch on a boat that left New York Harbor and traveled down the Intracoastal Waterway to Haiti. Dad and the witch secretly slipped down the stairs with me, trying not to attract the attention of my mother. Dad was on one side of me and the witch was on the other. We walked quietly down the stairs without saying a word. Dad already had the car waiting just outside the door, and he planned to whisk me away before my mother discovered I was gone.

But thankfully, his plan failed. God placed my mother in the right spot at the right time, and she walked around the corner before we could get to the bottom of the stairs. She looked up and saw the two of them with me and the suitcase. Startled, she demanded to know, "Where are you taking my baby?"

The witch shrieked, "This is not your baby! He's my baby!"

"You've lost your mind! He's my baby!" my mother shouted.

My mother and the witch engaged in a tug of war, with each one grabbing an arm and pulling me. Dad could not understand why my mother was upset. "If I send him to Haiti, he'll be rich! So what are you worried about?" Dad slapped my mother until she fell to the ground. I don't remember what happened immediately after that, but the next thing I recall is that Dad and the witch had left the house and I was still there with my mother. With God's intervention, I was protected and never sent to Haiti.

Dad was gone a few days and the witch never returned. Unfortunately she did not take the evil spirits with her, so that was not the end of the torment. Nor was it the end of the training. Dad and a demonic spirit—some would call it a spirit guide—kept teaching me voodoo. Here is how I was introduced to the demonic spirit guide.

After the witch left, I was asleep one night until I heard a loud noise that sounded like somebody dragging metal across the floor. It had the same effect as hundreds of fingernails being scraped across a blackboard. The worst fear of my life came over me. My brother and I shared a bed, so I was lying next to him, frozen in fear. My head was under the covers; when I peeked from under the covers, a demonic spirit was standing next to my bed and looking down at me. It said, "I am here to teach you."

"Go away!" I ordered. "Go away!"

The spirit kept repeating, "Go to Darien. You need to learn something in Darien." I did not understand what this spirit was trying to tell me, but later I learned that there are many witch covens in that part of Connecticut. I didn't go to Darien, so the evil spirit taught me what those witches could not.

Through all of this involvement with the occult, I had become so possessed by demonic spirits that I could levitate off the ground. I could make my spirit leave my body and travel to another location. Glass would not cut me. On one occasion, a spirit called pillardoc came into my room and said, "I control the money in the world. Come with me. I want to show you something." This spirit actually took me through a glass window pane and carried me up into some type of vision. He showed me Wall Street, banks, and a golden temple. This spirit said, "I can teach you how to rob banks. I can even teach you how to get in and out without being noticed. I can make one person rich and another person poor. Some see me as mammon. Don't trust God. Trust me."

The spirit took me back to my room through the glass window. My reaction was fascination. In those days I idolized Willie Sutton, the bank robber who could crack a safe and nobody knew how to stop him. At that time he was still robbing banks. I thought to myself, "If this spirit could just show me how to get in the building and come out the other side, the cops couldn't get me." I entertained the thought briefly. But I was still young enough to have fear of being out there all alone robbing banks.

One day after my father had beaten me badly, I went outside and stood in a field between two buildings that were about eight stories high. I looked up into the sky above the tops of the buildings and saw a city. At first I thought it was heaven, so I was very excited. I saw a person who looked like he had a crown on his head. He asked me, "Do you want to come up here?"

I replied, "Yes. I'm tired of these beatings."

"You'll have to do what I tell you to do," he said.

I agreed, and this person—who was not a person but a demonic spirit—gave me orders and told me what to do in the neighborhood. I didn't understand at the time that I was seeing demonic principalities of the air that ruled over the area where we lived. These spirits are dispatching spirits. They direct other spirits to go forth and wreck your business, your church, your home, your marriage, and your life. They leave everything in disarray.

These demonic spirits live in the air above the territory that they rule. In Ephesians, the Apostle Paul called them spiritual hosts of wickedness in heavenly places. He referred to Satan as the prince of the power of the air. These spirits operate like a government over that part of the earth. And they use people as their puppets; they attach strings to you and manipulate you, just like a puppeteer. You are never free to make a deal with the devil unless there are strings attached.

I don't want to talk much about the things I did at the order of these demonic spirits. I'm not proud of it. But I will say that I set homes on fire, put curses on people, and caused havoc in the neighborhood. I was so evil that people grabbed their children and ran into their homes when they saw "that Kelley boy" coming down the street.

Here I was, not yet a teenager and my life was being destroyed by demonic spirits, all because I had an evil voodoo priest for a father. Dad's influence on me continued to be destructive. Between teaching me voodoo and beating me constantly, he was turning me into a morally depraved boy. After one particular beating, one of my brothers finally had enough. He confronted Dad and said, "I'm sick of the way you treat him. You beat him every day and I'm tired of it."

Dad cursed as he yelled at my brother, "You don't tell me what to do!"

"You beat him and he doesn't do anything to deserve it. I won't allow you to beat him anymore!"

Before we knew what was happening, Dad had pulled a knife and cut my brother across his stomach. My brother shouted to me, "Run, Kurt, run! He's trying to kill both of us!"

I ran out of the house as quickly as I could. I had never been so afraid for my life. I knew that if this man would attack the person who was trying to protect me that he would surely kill me.

Since I feared going back home, I stayed with my mother's best friend. Dad could not find me; but since I showed up at their door with a bloody head, this family called the child protective agency and reported him. Agents went to the house and talked to Dad, and that is when the beatings slowed down. They didn't stop, but they were not as frequent after that.

This was not the first time I had run away from home. Once I ran to New York City and lived with drug dealers. I stayed there until one of the guys overdosed. When I saw him dead with the needle stuck in his arm, I pulled the needle out. His sisters saw me and thought I had killed their brother. They told me that they were going to kill me, too.

I tried to defend myself by telling them, "He shot his own heroin. I didn't do that. All I did was pull the needle out of his arm."

Still they were determined to make me pay. The two sisters and one other guy armed themselves with weapons and cornered me in the house. Miraculously, I was able to walk right past them and out the door as they stood as frozen as carved blocks of ice. There is no doubt in my mind that it was my mother's prayers and an angel of God that paralyzed the three of them and allowed me to leave that house safely. Thank God again for the powerful impact of the prayers of a righteous mother!

CHAPTER 3

Turning Around and Turning Back

"Afterward Jesus found him in the temple and said to him, 'See, you have been made well. Sin no more, lest a worse thing come upon you.' "
- John 5:14

Life was so miserable at home that sometimes I ran away and slept on park benches. Anything was better than staying in a house with my dad. Even though I ran away several times, I always went back home. Dad's beatings didn't stop completely until I was thirteen years old. By that time I was carrying a pistol, and I told Dad that I would shoot and kill him if he ever touched me again. "Hit me again," I dared him. "Go ahead. Hit me. It'll be your last time. You'll never beat me again because I'll kill you if you touch me."

At thirteen, I accepted a job protecting prostitutes for a pimp, which is why I carried a pistol. I protected the women of a New York pimp, but I was upset with this guy because he beat his girls and took all their money. They couldn't even afford to buy food or coats. I was so angry over the way he treated the girls that I wanted to see him in a pool of blood. I made plans to shoot him and push him out a window. It was surely the mercy of God that kept me away from that pimp. I stopped working for him when Tony, a friend of mine who was the pimp for his own sister, asked me to protect his women.

Most of the girls I knew who became prostitutes were lacking a father figure. They were looking for a man to be their daddy. The prostitutes who stroll the streets are almost always addicted to drugs, and prostitution becomes a way to pay for their drug habit.

It was never a surprise when another body of a dead prostitute was delivered to the coroner's office. Sometimes they died from a drug overdose and other times a customer killed them. People who hire prostitutes or engage in prostitution can become possessed by many demonic spirits. And when the spirit that causes hate possesses them, a customer will think nothing of strangling a prostitute to death. I was hired to protect the pimp's prostitutes from killers. I was also told, "Don't forget. You've got the gun. If they don't pay, kill them."

Eventually I had to stop working that job because I thought I was going to lose my mind. A thirteen-year-old does not need to be in that kind of environment. I was already tormented by demonic spirits, addicted to drugs, and living in hell at home. I was always at risk of being killed by rival gang members. My life was in shambles, and watching acts of prostitution several times a night became more than I could handle.

Sometimes I went into Brooklyn and sat alone on a park bench just to get relief. One time I left New York and had gotten off the train when a young white boy approached me and said, "Hey nigger, where you going?"

"I'm going home."

He ran in front of me and said, "No you're not. Hey, daddy, shoot that nigger!" His dad pulled a gun that looked like a 45-magnum.

"What did I do to you?" I asked.

"You can't walk on this sidewalk. We own this sidewalk."

He put the gun to my head, but each time he pulled the trigger, nothing happened. I faced them and took my time walking backwards as I told the two of them that I would be back to kill them.

My life was filled with close calls. Once I was at this same train station when I was nearly hit by a bullet train. I knew the train was coming down the track, but I heard the same voice that spoke to me at age four as it said, "Run across the track! You can make it! You can outrun it! Go! Run across the track!"

There were four tracks to cross, and some of the trains moved slowly. But the Boston Union bullet train traveled from Boston to Washington, D.C. at about a hundred miles an hour. It was fast and made almost no noise.

I obeyed the voice that told me to run. I started across the track and here came the bullet train. Just as I lifted my foot off the last track, the speeding train covered the ground where I had been standing.

Then there was the incident with the giant snapping turtle. I was sitting at the Connecticut River one hot day with my feet dangling in the water when I heard a voice say, "Kurt!" I looked around and didn't see anybody. The voice kept calling, "Kurt!" Still I didn't see anybody. But an invisible hand pulled me away from the water just as a giant snapping turtle came out of the water and headed straight for my foot. These turtles are huge, and when they bite, they pull their prey under the water. God saved me from an attack, and perhaps from drowning that day.

When I was about thirteen years old, Dad enrolled me in Stamford's junior police force. Since I was a thug, Dad thought I needed structure and more torment. The moment I walked in the room that first day, the other students taunted me with, "Ghetto trash! Project trash!" They all lived in the better parts of town, and apparently they were not accustomed to having people from my side of town in their junior police force. A Puerto Rican girl walked into the class and they treated her the same way. She reacted by crying, but I said, "Don't let them get to you.

They call us ghetto trash, but we'll show them. We'll band together and show these rich kids that they can't look down on us."

I set a goal to make sergeant in two months. Besides impressing the rich kids, I knew that my dad put me in this force to punish me, so I was determined to show him what I was capable of accomplishing. They taught us to march, turn, pivot, spin, throw a rifle in the air and catch it, and spin the rifle around our necks. Although we wore uniforms and earned stripes, we were not learning police techniques; we were simply learning to perform in parades.

The ridicule continued. "Ghetto trash! Project trash!" The Puerto Rican girl was overweight, so she also had to deal with being called names because of her weight.

"Hang in there," I encouraged her. "We'll stick together and do this. We'll show them we're not ghetto trash." She and I worked hard, and we even stayed after class and practiced. After we had been in the force for two months, she and I received our sergeant stripes. Nobody else in the class achieved that rank in two months. But do you think that made my father proud?

In this class I had to deal with boys—particularly the instructor's son—who wanted to pick fights with me. Some were taller and heavier than I was at that time. I could hold my own in a fight, but I also knew that I couldn't fight somebody who was twice my size by hitting him in the upper body. I had to hit him low to knock him off his center of gravity. One guy often used lunges to knock me down while nobody else was looking. He came after me one day during the training class with a football rolling block. He rushed toward me like a rhinoceros, but when he had almost reached me, I dropped to the ground. He hit me, lost his balance, and skidded across the blacktop. He was friendly toward me after that, probably because he was afraid of me.

I stayed in the junior police force until I could no longer deal with my friends in our neighborhood making fun of me. Nobody wanted to be around me anymore because they thought I was a real cop. Being in the junior police force was not an honor in my neighborhood, so I dropped out.

From a young age, I had a reputation for being a fighter. I was very young when I put on my first pair of sixteen ounce boxing gloves that were almost as big as my head and boxed a guy named Dodge Harris. Since we lived in the projects, some of my fighting was dirty street fighting. We had private clubs where we engaged in bare knuckle fighting.

One day in downtown Stamford I noticed a boxing gym. As I walked past, I heard the sound of punching bags and looked inside the door out of curiosity. A boxing ring was set up, and a man was in the middle of the ring shadow boxing.

When he looked up and saw me he said, "I know who you are. You're a good street fighter. Why don't you come in and let me train you to be a pro?"

I declined the offer at first but he insisted. Before long I found myself at this gym, learning to punch with power and jab at lightening fast speed. By the time I finished training with this man, my street fighting looked amateurish. I could knock somebody down with a single jab.

In seventh grade I joined a nationwide amateur organization for teenage boxers called the Golden Gloves. We were matched with other boxers according to weight and skill level, and we boxed in tournaments against members from other regional clubs. In the Golden Gloves, you feel like a pro boxer, although you don't fight like a professional. Seldom do they let you knock someone out.

The Golden Gloves is a potential gateway to the Olympics, and from there to professional boxing. Almost every professional boxer first won tournaments with the Golden Gloves. Men like George Foreman, Joe Lewis, Joe Frazier, Evander Holyfield, and Sugar Ray Leonard moved from the Golden Gloves to professional boxing. Even though I didn't make the Olympics, my training at this gym and my experience with the Golden Gloves gave me an edge over other fighters. The training would also help me years later when I became a professional heavyweight boxer.

The children in our family didn't get to attend church often because Dad refused to let our mother take us along. But when Dad wasn't around to stop her, or when he was too drunk to put up a fight, our mother took us along to the church she attended. I knew enough about God and Christianity to know that the things I was doing were wrong. They had to be wrong. But I had no inclination to change my lifestyle and give my heart to Christ. Besides, why would God want me after the life I had been living?

During one of Dad's drunken spells, Mom took us to a church in Stamford called the Little Zion Church of God in Christ. I was a heathen, of course, but I still loved church because it gave me a break from my dad and from the streets. I hated to see the service end because it meant I had to go back into that environment.

On this particular day I was sitting in the church beside my brother Richard. I heard a voice in the back of the sanctuary saying, "Kurt! Kurt!"

I looked around and didn't see anybody. I said to my brother Richard, "Somebody's calling my name."

"Nobody's calling you," he replied.

I heard the voice again. "Kurt! I'm going to use you! You're going to do great things for God!" I was accustomed to hearing voices, but this voice didn't sound like the others. I could tell it was not trying to hurt me. It even sounded as though it loved me. Other than my mother, I did not sense that anybody loved me as a child. This voice intrigued me, and I had no fear when I heard this voice speak.

The voice continued to call my name, and I finally got up and went to the back of the church to look under the pews. I wanted to see who was talking to me. Nobody was there. Then the voice said, "Go to the altar. I have chosen you to do a special work."

Conviction hit me and I went to the altar. I repented of my sins and gave my life to Christ that day. The glory of God was all over me, and I knew it was the Lord. I said, "What do you want me to do, Lord?"

"Just start praising me," was His answer.

So I did; I praised God and cried out to Him. I knew that I wanted to be good for a change. I wanted to have a different lifestyle. Once again I heard the voice, but this time it said, "You are going to minister for me. I'm going to use you to do a great work for me some day."

Bishop I. L. Jefferson, a distant cousin on my mother's side and the Bishop over the Church of God in Christ for the state of Connecticut, was at the church that night. When I opened my eyes after praying at the altar, Bishop Jefferson was standing beside me. He said, "God has saved you. He has called you to do great works for Him. I might not be here to see it, but you're going to do great works."

"Me?" I asked.

"Yes. God is going to use you."

I fell in love with the Lord that night. When I walked home from church, I felt so light that it seemed I was walking on a cloud. I walked through the house praising and thanking the Lord. No evil spirits could torment me. Not one spirit in the house could touch me that night. Even Dad stayed away from me and stopped beating me. In fact, it seemed that I was invisible to him and he couldn't touch me.

My dreams changed and I slept well at night for the first time since I was five years old. I was instantly delivered from drugs with no withdrawal symptoms. Normally when you come off drugs, it feels like a thousand worms are digging and chewing through your skin. I thank God that He delivered me instantly.

People in my neighborhood noticed a change in me. Even those who worked in the gambling den knew that something about me was different. Miss Jeanette, who ran the gambling den said, "Kirky, something's different about you. What is it?"

I told her, "I went to church and got saved. Miss Jeanette, God wants to save you, too."

After seeing the change in my life, Miss Jeanette said, "If God can save somebody like you, then He can do something for me." She accepted Christ and turned her life around. She lived for the Lord until she died.

Everywhere I went, people wanted to know what happened to me. I told them I got saved, and many of them accepted Christ because they saw such a vast improvement in my life.

One day I was at my grandmother's house, telling her how happy I was that the Lord had saved me. Her house was about a block from our house and I left, still praising and thanking God that I no longer had to deal with demons, witchcraft, or drugs. I was walking down the sidewalk and the sun was shining. A brilliant light, brighter than the sun, appeared and surrounded me. I heard a voice say, "You have been chosen. You have been chosen to do a mighty work." The light lasted no more than a few moments, but it seemed that it lasted hours.

Finally I was turning my life around and getting on the right track. But the enemy doesn't give up easily. Satan was already forming a plan to get me back.

I had a sporadic relationship with one girl at that time, and she was the only girl who was remotely interested in me. She was a positive influence on me, and she often told me how I needed to get off drugs and turn my life around. She was always in my corner, fighting to keep me alive and off drugs.

But after I accepted Christ, I was bombarded with girls who seemed to be interested in me. Girls I didn't even know were calling me five times a day and asking if I wanted to attend a party with them.

"No, I don't want to go to a party," I replied.

"Want to go to a club?"

"No, I don't want to go to a club."

I ignored the girls and told them I was not interested in them or their parties. But they kept calling. They persisted until they wore me down. I started going to clubs and parties with these girls and did the very thing the Davis brothers did. I turned my back on God.

Once I returned to a life of sin, the girls disappeared. Not one of them ever called me again; nor would they return my phone calls. I ignored the only girl who once had been a positive influence in my life, and I allowed strange women to pull me away from God. The Bible says that, when an evil spirit leaves a man, the spirit roams through dry places, seeking rest. When he finds none, he returns to the house from which he came. If the house has been cleaned and put in order, the spirit returns with seven other spirits more wicked than himself, and they will try to enter the house and dwell there. If they succeed, the last state of that person will be worse than the first.

This scripture tells us that, when God saves us, evil spirits are forced to leave. We start cleaning up our life. But each spirit that was forced to leave will try to return, bringing along seven other spirits that are even more wicked. If we turn our back on God and return to sin and bondage, we will be much worse off than before. The attacks of the enemy will be greater, and we will slide deeper into sin. That is exactly what happened to me. When I backslid away from the Lord, I became more wicked than I had been before I accepted Christ.

This time I started killing animals, usually cats. I set homes on fire while people were inside. I tried to choke people to death. Before I accepted Christ, I had already seen several different demonic spirits manifest in the visible realm, but now I was seeing spirits that I had not seen before. I saw the run-ahead demon, which can be dispatched to run ahead of you and cause trouble. When I planned to go someplace where I wanted attention diverted from me before I arrived, I ordered this spirit to run ahead of me and wreak havoc. When I arrived at my intended destination, the people were so focused on their troubles that they hardly noticed I was there. I could look around the room and see this spirit laughing at the disaster it had created.

I saw another strange-looking demonic spirit on the street one day. A friend in my neighborhood asked me to attend a party with her in another neighborhood. I didn't want to go for two reasons. First, the party was being held in another neighborhood and I risked being attacked by rival gang members. Second, she told me that she also expected me to have sex with her. Through my voodoo training, I already knew about transference of spirits, and I knew the kinds of spirits that attach themselves to people who have sex outside of marriage. Even as a sinner, I wanted no part of that. I had enough problems and I didn't need to be possessed by any of those demonic spirits.

I told the girl I wouldn't go. She persisted, so I said, "Okay, I'll go. But I'm not sleeping with you." We had walked about ten feet down the street when I saw a creature that seemed to be standing in a tree. The bottom half looked like a tree trunk, but the top was a demonic spirit.

Addressing me it said, "I control all the drugs. Come over here to me. I want to tell you things you don't know. I want to give you something that will make you more powerful. I can put you over this whole area. Come here. Come closer to me."

Aloud I said, "No! No, I'm not coming closer to you!"

"Come here! Come here!" it insisted.

"No, I won't come near you!"

Keep in mind that the girl I was with could neither see nor hear what was happening in the spirit realm, so she thought I was talking to her. She pulled my arm and asked, "What's the matter? What's wrong with you?"

The spirit kept talking. "Come here! I will give you more knowledge of drugs than anybody in this whole neighborhood. You can be over the whole neighborhood. You can learn everything about drugs. Just let me get my hands on you, and all the knowledge that is in me will come into you."

I already knew as much as I wanted to know about drugs, but this spirit wanted to teach me even more. I was so frightened that I refused to walk down the street any further. I would not risk passing that spirit because I didn't want that thing to get its hands on me.

The killings, rapes, drugs, beatings, witchcraft, and all the evil and mayhem in our neighborhood finally became more than my mother could handle. The area was becoming increasingly dangerous and many of my friends were dying. We watched as one person committed suicide and many others died of a drug overdose. One was shot in the neck when he tried to rob a liquor store. Yet another was killed by the police. I sometimes saw a dingy yellow light appear on my friends, as though a dirty flashlight was shining in their faces. Each time I saw that light, the person died. When I realized their death followed, I would see the light and think, "Oh, no. Not Lisa." And Lisa would die. Then I'd see the yellow light on another friend and think, "Oh, no. Not Clint. He's so smart, but the light is on him, too." Then Clint would die. One by one, fifty-four of our friends died prematurely.

Our neighborhood in Stamford had become a portal to hell. There is no question that the children in our family survived because my mother's prayers protected every one of us. She often spoke over us, "Not one of my children will die prematurely. God promised me that all of my children will be saved, and great is the salvation of my children."

My mother sensed that God was telling her to get out of Stamford for the protection of her children. Dad refused to leave. So one day while Dad was at work, Mom assigned children to each room and we quickly packed up our belongings, loaded them into a moving van, and left for Milwaukee without telling Dad where we were going. I was fifteen years old at the time.

When we arrived in Milwaukee we lived with our cousin Virgie Houston, who was related to Bishop Jefferson in Connecticut. They had ten children, and we all lived together in their large home. Even with so many people in the house, we all got along very well and never even argued.

I was in culture shock when we moved to Wisconsin. In Stamford, we had New York City right around the corner. I was familiar with Manhattan, Queens, Harlem, Greenwich Village, and Central Park. Dozens of different languages were spoken in my neighborhood alone. Milwaukee was quite a change from a big city on the east coast. There were no tall buildings, no subway, no parks, and the police couldn't be bought off. The girls were not tough like New York women. The streets were immaculate and we didn't live in the projects.

My mother was thrilled that we could no longer deal drugs. What she didn't know was that we could now get our drugs from Chicago. The Kelley boys did not change their ways; in no time, we were back to our old habits of dealing and using drugs. My brothers also worked as pimps. Somehow we managed to do this from their house, right under their noses, without Mom and Virgie knowing about it.

My sister, Chandler, tried her best to get me to attend church. She said, "Kirk, God has been good to you. He has spared your life many times and He wants to save your soul."

All the while, I was thinking, "I can't get saved right now. We have a big shipment of cocaine coming in from Chicago and I'm going to be making a lot of money. I wish she'd shut up."

I was fifteen years old but had lived the life of a man three times my age. My childhood had been wrecked. I had learned and practiced voodoo, used drugs, worked as a pimp's bodyguard, and seen fifty-four of my friends die. People had pulled guns on me more times than I could count. I had been attacked by rival gang members. I had escaped many chances to die lost and go straight to hell. In fact, I thought my life *was* hell. But I had not truly experienced hell. Very soon, I was going to learn what hell was really like.

CHAPTER 4

A Trip to Hell

"Let death seize them; let them go down alive into hell, for wickedness is in their dwellings and among them."
- Psalm 55:15

One hot summer day in 1971, my brother Bobby and his friend Bill decided to go to a bar along the waterfront.

"Can I go, too?" I asked.

"No. You're too young."

They planned to leave within an hour and head to the bar. In the meantime, I heard a voice—that same voice I heard in Stamford, Connecticut at the age of four. This time it was a very enthusiastic voice that said, "All these years you've been getting high. But it doesn't last long. You need to get super-high. You've never been really high. Why don't you try getting super-high?"

I had always wanted more of everything, so the idea of experiencing a greater high appealed to me. I was willing to do whatever the voice told me to do. Just like the African hunters who dig a hole and cover it with branches and sticks while waiting for the animal to walk by and fall into the trap, so it was with me. The enemy had dug a pit, covered it up to make it appear safe, and was waiting for me to fall into the trap like a hunted animal.

The voice instructed me, "Get your weed, your cocaine, and some pills."

I obeyed and put the drugs in my pocket. The pills I chose were strong enough to keep you high for days. I pocketed about five hundred dollars worth of cocaine. Mixing all of those drugs is called a speed ball, and it will most likely cause your heart to stop. People who do this nearly always die of a drug overdose.

I talked Bobby and Bill into taking me to the bar with them. I hopped in the back seat of the car and smoked a joint of marijuana. The voice said, "Drop the drugs. Go ahead. You've never mixed all those drugs together before. Take all of them."

As I sat in the back seat smoking marijuana, I took the rest of the drugs. By the time we arrived at Lake Michigan, I was so high that I was staggering when I got out of the car. Bobby and Bill laughed because they thought it was hilarious. I was proud to show them what a man I was.

My head was buzzing like a bee as we walked past the loading docks where cranes were lifting crates off the ships. We walked into a small bar where several men were drinking beer and shooting pool. I sat down at the bar to the left of Bobby and Bill. I had no plans to drink beer because I hated beer. Besides, I was underage. But that didn't matter to the bartender.

As he wiped glasses and served drinks, the bartender looked at me and said, "What will you have?"

"I don't drink," I replied.

"You'll drink if you sit at my bar."

"Then give me a beer."

To my surprise, he sat one in front of me. As I sipped the beer, I could feel the effects of all those drugs kicking in. I felt myself experiencing the super-high that the spirit told me about. The sun was shining through the window and hitting me on the head. The music was playing in the background and I was rocking back and forth. I was feeling pretty good.

But before long I started sweating profusely. My heart was beating so rapidly that I was certain it was going to explode. In the snap of a finger, everything on either side of me turned black. I could still see the sun coming through the window and the bartender standing in front of me, but everything to the sides of me was dark.

Then I noticed that the rays of sun that had been shining on my face shifted. No longer was the sun shining on my face. Instead, the rays came toward me but moved around my head. I moved to another chair so the sun's rays would hit me; but again, the rays bent around my head. I know it sounds impossible, but the sun would no longer shine on me. The rays actually moved *around* my head. Even the natural sun cannot pierce that kind of gross darkness. Soon all of the light disappeared and everything in front of and around me turned black. I was sitting in darkness. I have never spent much time in a cave, but it seemed that I was surrounded by the kind of darkness you would experience in a cave.

I realized I was overdosing and thought, "What have I done? Why did I listen to that voice?" Panic struck me.

Then I saw spirits—perhaps fifty of them—come out of the floor. They had no faces, but their heads were shaped like cones. They were black and of a variety of sizes. They all grabbed me and hit me like we were in a huddle. I stood up and pleaded with Bobby and Bill to take me home.

Both laughed and said, "Oh, you can't hold your drugs. Get back over there and sit down."

"No! You've got to take me home!" I knew that if I could get home, my mother would put some of that anointing oil on my head and pray for me and everything would be all right.

"We're not taking you home. Get back over there and sit down!"

The spirits had completely surrounded me. I could still hear conversations and music, but I could no longer hear a complete conversation. Instead, I could hear every few words, as though the volume was being turned up and down.

"Take me home! You've got to take me home!" I shouted in desperation.

"What's wrong with you? Can't you hold your drugs?"

I kept pleading with them until they reluctantly agreed to take me home. They helped me into the back seat of the car and they sat in the front, complaining the whole time about having to take me home. As I lay in the back seat, the spirits grabbed me again. This time, they snatched me out of my body and pulled me through the floor of the car. I saw the drive shaft underneath the car; then the spirits pulled me into the earth. As I traveled through the earth, I saw sewer pipes, rocks, and everything else that was inside the earth. I was dragged to a place in the earth that was red and black. Then the spirits dropped me to the bottom of a floor.

Demonic spirits beat me on the head and laughed as they mockingly said, "You did voodoo for us. You were a sorcerer. You sold drugs for us. We tricked you! Now you're in hell. You can't get out of here. You belong to us now. You're lost forever!" They continued to laugh at me, mock me, and remind me of every bad thing I had ever done. They tormented me in ways that I don't want to talk about in this book.

The only thought that came to mind was, "I guess this is what I get for all the bad things I've done. I'm stuck now and there's nothing I can do about it."

The spirits finally let me go, and I saw a road ahead that had a yellow line down the center. I took off running as the spirits laughed and taunted me, "Go ahead and run! Take off! Run as fast as you can!"

I ran, thinking that perhaps I could get to the road and find my way back out. But when I got to the road, I discovered that it was nothing but a wall with a yellow line painted on it.

The spirits laughed, grabbed me, and tormented me all over again. They beat me in the head with some kind of sledgehammer. Hideous and deformed demonic spirits of every size imaginable had a hold on me, and they did to me whatever they wanted. The torment was nonstop. I had no defense against them, and there was no place to run or hide.

It seemed that every bad thing I had ever done, every good thing I had ever heard about Jesus, every Sunday School lesson I'd been taught, and every prayer I'd heard my mother pray came back to me. But there was not one thing I could do about it now. I was in hell.

Suddenly two hands that were a golden color and brighter than the noonday sun came down into this room where I was being tormented. The demonic spirits saw them, too, and they screamed, "No! No! He belongs to us! You can't have him! No!"

The hands grabbed me by the shoulders and pulled me out of hell. The demonic spirits tried unsuccessfully to grab me by my feet. I came back up the same way I went down. Again I saw the earth, the rocks, the sewer pipes of the city, and the spinning drive shaft of the car. The thought came to me, "How am I going to get through the bottom of this car?" But my spirit went through the car, and the golden hands put me back into my body.

Bobby and Bill were still in the front seat, completely unaware that I had died. I could barely hear, and my vision was blurry from the drug overdose. I was so thankful to be out of hell that the only thought crossing my mind was, "Oh, thank you God. I'm out of hell. But I'm going to be deaf for the rest of my life." Almost as quickly as I had that thought, my hearing was restored to normal and I could hear the guys in the front seat cursing me for not being able to hold my drugs.

I lay on the seat and thought, "Oh, God. I've been to hell. I've been to hell! I am so thankful to be out of hell."

A voice spoke to me and said, "Because of your mother's prayers, and because you have been chosen by God, you were spared."

At that moment, I realized the power of my mother's prayers. Had my mother not been a praying woman—a woman who anointed us, blessed us, and persistently prayed over us—I'm sure I would have died at the age of fifteen from a drug overdose. I would have been tormented in hell for eternity. Thank God for His grace and mercy! And thank God for a praying mother.

Bobby pulled up to the curb in front of our house where he and Bill dragged me out of the car, dropped me at the curb, and drove off. I was unable to move my legs because the drugs had damaged some of my nerves. I crawled to the front door using my upper torso. My sister came outside and screamed when she saw me lying outside the door. I do not remember the ride to the hospital, but when I arrived, they put me in the mental ward.

That was before the days of drug and alcohol rehabilitation facilities. The ward had bars on the windows. People screamed constantly. I heard them shouting things like, "Stop them! Make them leave me alone!" I lay in bed and thought, "What am I doing here with these crazy people?"

My mother finally told the hospital that she was coming to pick me up and take me home. The doctors reluctantly agreed to let me leave. I was still partially blind and could not walk, so I had to be rolled to the car in a wheelchair. My family had to carry me from the car to my bed.

For the next month, I was in terrible shape. I was paralyzed from the waist down and had to wear adult diapers.

One night around midnight, I closed my eyes and thought about where I was and how I got there. I knew there was a God but I didn't know whether or not to thank Him for saving me from hell. I was lying in bed with a thankful heart, but I wasn't necessarily thanking God. I was just thinking, "Oh, my God. I was in hell. I was in hell. I'm so thankful to be out of hell." I didn't believe God would have saved me from hell because I was an evil person. Why would God think enough of me to save me from hell?

While I was lying there with my eyes closed, I suddenly felt like I was floating through the clouds like an airplane. A small cherub appeared in my head; it was not a dream because I was not asleep. I spoke to this cherub and said, "What are you doing here? You're in the wrong house. I'm a sorcerer." Then I opened my eyes and saw that the cherub was in the room with me!

The cherub replied, "I was sent from the throne of God to protect you."

"To protect *me*? You were sent here to protect *me*?"

"Yes, to protect *you*. And yes, you were in hell."

Naming one of the demonic spirits I had seen in hell, the cherub explained to me, "This spirit goes throughout hell supervising the torment of people. He is coming to take you back to hell. But do not fear. I am here to protect you."

The cherub blended into the corner of my room and went through the ceiling as he said, "Do not fear. Do not fear."

As the cherub disappeared, I became fearful and cried, "Don't leave! Stay here with me!"

Suddenly I heard a loud commotion in the room next to me. It sounded as though somebody was smashing windows and turning over furniture. I was certain someone had broken into the house, but I couldn't do anything since I was paralyzed from the waist down.

My dog Blackie, a giant schnauzer, sensed something because the hair on his back stood up and he began to growl. Into my room walked a demonic creature that was muddy gray with a smooth body that appeared to be made from clay. His teeth were pointed and his eyes were extremely large for his face. He held a stick in his hand as he said, "I've searched the annals of hell looking for you, but you were not there. Somehow you got out. I'm coming to take you back."

I wanted to protect myself, and even Blackie continued to bark and growl as he jumped between me and the spirit. Every time the spirit moved, my dog blocked his path. It seemed as though there was an invisible wall between me and this demonic spirit. Finally the spirit said to me, "I can't get you. You are protected. I can't take you back." Then he turned and walked out the door.

Before I realized what I was doing, I jumped out of bed and ran to the other room. I had not walked from the time my brother dropped me off in the yard after the drug overdose. Yet here I was, jumping out of bed and running to the other room. It dawned on me that I was no longer paralyzed.

When I reached the other room, I expected to see windows broken, furniture overturned, and the house a wreck after the noise I heard before the spirit entered my room. But nothing was disturbed. I wondered if the cherub made the demonic spirit straighten the place up on his way back to hell. I also wondered if it was the power of God that came into the room with the cherub that allowed me to get out of bed and walk.

Days later, my sister Chandler invited me to a revival. She kept telling me, "Kirk, you need to go to church and straighten up your life. God has been so good to you and now you've turned your back on Him."

I didn't particularly want to go to church right away because I wanted to make money on the shipment of cocaine that was coming in from Chicago. I was good at cutting the cocaine and adding Johnson's foot powder and Ajax (a dealer never sells pure cocaine on the streets), and that was still the only thing I had on my mind. There were a lot of potential customers in the area who had never tried cocaine, so we knew that we could remove a significant amount of money from their wallets by getting them hooked on a new drug.

But Chandler stayed in my face and pestered me constantly. I told her, "Leave me along! I'm not going to church and getting saved!" But Chandler was on fire for the Lord and she was quite a soul winner. She came into my room one day and said, "Kirk, forget about that shipment of cocaine. You will never see any of that dope or any of that money. You are going to church with me and getting saved." She was so persistent that I finally went just to get her off my back.

Chandler and another sister carried me into the church by one getting under each arm. The service was great and the minister preached a fiery sermon. People were praising God in the aisles. After church I told Chandler, "That was a good service but I won't be going back." She insisted that I return the following night.

So I did. Again they carried me into the church. My legs felt like wet noodles and I still couldn't walk very well. I also had not recovered from the nerve damage that caused me to lose control of my bowels, so I was still wearing adult diapers.

During the service that night, the pastor stopped in the middle of his message and pointed his finger at me. He said, "You, the young man back there, come up here." Everybody turned around to look and so did I. But when I turned around, there was nothing behind me except the wall. I realized he was talking to me. Again he said, "Young man, come up here."

Then I heard a voice say to me, "I love you," and it told me everything I had been through, including my recent trip to hell. "It was God who saved your soul from hell," the voice said. "He loves you and He has a plan for your life. You will testify of all the things He has brought you through. Walk to the altar."

The enemy tried to keep me away from the altar by telling me that my legs wouldn't carry me to the altar. He tried to convince me that I might have an accident because I could not control my bowels. "Don't do it," the enemy said.

But the Lord said, "Come to me. Come now. I will save you."

I stood to walk to the altar. It felt like my legs were not going to carry my one hundred fifty-five pound frame, but with each step I took, God added strength to my limbs. When I reached the altar, the minister told me everything I had been through in the past.

"God wants to save you tonight," the minister told me. "Do you want to receive Him now?"

"Yes, yes, I do," I replied. That night, on December 15, 1971, I repented of my sins and gave my life back to Jesus. When I did, it felt as though a pile of trash had been washed off me. As I prayed with my arms raised toward heaven, I saw a hand that was surrounded by blue and yellow fire come through the ceiling and touch my head. The hand seemed to go inside my head. The moment it did, I received the baptism of the Holy Spirit and began speaking in tongues. I saw a vision of myself preaching around the world in countries that I had only read about in school.

I thought to myself, "Cool. Just show me how." God also completely healed me from all the nerve damage I suffered from the drug overdose.

Shortly after I rededicated my life to Christ, I was lying on the couch one night, thanking God and speaking in tongues. Suddenly I felt my spirit coming off the couch, going through the roof, and out into the darkness of the universe. I traveled quickly and then stopped. Surrounding me were beautiful mountains and trees, and everything was incredibly peaceful. I was no longer in darkness; in fact, it was so bright that I was looking for the sun but did not see it.

I saw the silhouettes of two people who were speaking in a language I could not understand. Then I heard them speaking English. I wish I could hear it all again because I can't remember everything they said. But they were talking about me. They said, "He is going to minister for us. He will go around the world for us and people are going to be delivered. People will be saved and set free."

When I saw this scene I said, "Please let me stay. I've suffered all my life. I've been beaten, abused, and tormented. Let me stay. Please let me stay." I saw a beautiful gate a distance ahead of me and asked if I could go through the gate.

"No, not yet," was their reply. "You will be with us someday, but not now."

I returned to earth quickly. Darkness was under me as I came back into the night. My spirit went through the house and back into my body. What an experience that was! I felt like I was walking on a cloud for days afterward.

The enemy tried every trick possible to turn me back to a life of sin. But it wasn't going to work this time. After I rededicated my life to Christ, I started attending the Utopian Temple Church of God in Christ and learning the word of God. Pastor Joe Lee and Lucy Hughes were outstanding teachers. Pastor Lee taught us how to pray and fast. I remember the first time I heard about the sixth chapter of Ephesians where the Bible speaks of wrestling against principalities, powers, rulers of darkness, and spiritual hosts of wickedness in the heavenly places. My mind went back to the city I had seen in the sky when we lived in Stamford. I thought to myself, "I know who you're talking about. Those guys were evil. How did they get written up in the Bible?"

I didn't say much about my past experiences at that time; I just listened and learned. Pastor Lee taught us about deliverance and the power to overcome demonic spirits. I could relate to everything he was saying. He went on long fasts and cast demons out of people. There was a young man in our church who would give his life to Christ and then backslide. He would rededicate his life to Christ and backslide again. He did this over and over. One night his mother brought him to church and the pastor prayed for him. During the prayer, the boy's face changed to the appearance of a werewolf. He was so strong that he fought the nine men who had gathered to pray for him.

I received on-the-job deliverance training in that church. I was taught how to help people receive deliverance from the very spirits I had dealt with my whole life. I am so thankful that God put me in that church because I needed that teaching to learn to fight the enemy. Without that kind of teaching, I might have had a nice testimony but no knowledge or ability to use the power and authority of God. I believe God placed me in that church to enhance my own spiritual development. Pastor Lee is still alive and pastoring that same church. We are good friends today, and I consider him a tremendous man of God.

Our church held a year-long revival and, during that time, I became the church drummer. I had once played the bongo drums; so when the drummer left the church, they asked me to play the drums. One of the bass players took the time to teach me to play stick drums. You can't have a black church without an organ, a bass player, and a drummer! I became known throughout the whole state of Wisconsin as a talented drummer.

We had lived in Milwaukee about eight months when we moved into a big yellow house on Burleigh Street. Dad learned where we were and, when we came home from church one night, there was his car in our driveway. To our regret, he moved back in with us.

We already knew how shocked he had been to come home from work the day we moved out and find that we and most of the household belongings were gone. The neighbors watched through their windows and saw him open the door and drop to the floor. After we left, he told everybody his version of the story: "My wife left me and took the kids. I don't understand why they left. We got along very well and I never did a thing to them."

But in the eight months that we were gone, Dad had not fared well. His health declined rapidly and he was so ill with emphysema that he needed an oxygen tank to breathe. He was hospitalized once, and when he returned home, all of his hair had turned gray. He could barely get out of bed and he needed nursing care.

My mother was working in the nursing field again, but she could not care for him because she had to earn a living. One of my sisters brought a girl that I will call Linda into the house to care for Dad.

Linda looked Haitian, and although she was only two years older than I, she seemed much more mature. She cooked, cleaned the house, and cared for Dad. My sisters left everything in her hands and Dad became very fond of her.

I was not aware that, behind my back, Dad was trying to fix me up with this caretaker. He said to her, "Young lady, you've been so good to me. You will make somebody a good wife. I have five sons. Which one do you want?"

"Kirk," she replied.

"I've treated Kirk badly all his life. As my last wish, I want you to marry him. Promise me that you will make him happy."

"Don't worry, Mr. Kelley. I'll be the best wife he could ever have."

Dad often said to me, "Linda's a nice girl. I hope you'll marry her before I die."

This girl was not my type. Yes, she could cook. But I wasn't interested in marrying her. Still, my father was persistent. "Tell me that you'll marry this girl before I die," he kept insisting.

Just to get him off my back, I said, "Yeah, Dad. Okay. Sure, I'll marry her."

Milwaukee was bitter cold in the wintertime; on one occasion, the only place colder was Siberia. Dad couldn't handle the cold so he left the area in January of 1973 and moved to Tucson, Arizona where the weather was mild. He had family there, but none of us moved with him.

It was February 4, 1973 when Dad died. He had once been a handsome and strong man who weighed about two hundred pounds. When he died, he weighed ninety-eight pounds. And even though he was only fifty-six years old, he looked like an old man. He did not want to accept the nice suit that my mother gave him for Christmas, but he was buried in it. I cried when he died, but I did not attend his funeral.

Before a sinner dies, he or she will sometimes experience a fearsome spirit of death. Before Dad died, he was in his bedroom when he heard a noise that sounded like somebody trying to beat the house down. Then he heard the sound of hard breathing that reminded him of a bear. He also heard a dragging ball and chain.

I knew enough about the demonic spirit realm to know that Dad heard the evil spirit that had come to drag his soul and spirit away to hell. When a person dies who is full of hell, then hell itself comes after that person at death.

There is a death angel that God can send to slay thousands of people, as we read of in the Bible when God protected the children of Israel. But there is also a horrible, evil spirit that comes to carry away those who have lived a sinful life. Sometimes these people die in contorted positions, or they might have a look of torment on their faces. Before they die, some will scream when they see the spirit that is coming for them. And sadly, they are tormented even worse after death. For eternity, they will never have a moment of peace or rest.

Dad was a striking and intelligent man who knew the Bible from front to back. He could preach well enough to win contests in a Baptist church. Had he lived righteously and been obedient to the Lord, he could have been an outstanding man of God.

But Dad was foolish. He died for his unfaithfulness against the Lord. The book of Ecclesiastes tells us, "Do not be overly wicked, nor be foolish. Why should you die before your time?" There is no question that, at the age of fifty-six, my dad died before his time. My mother, on the other hand, is still alive today at the age of eighty-one. Her optical nerves are severed and she is blind from the beatings she suffered at the hands of my father. But otherwise, she is doing very well and is still on fire for God.

Sometimes I look back and wonder what might have happened had Dad lived longer. Could I have led him to a true relationship with the Lord? I've often thought that Mom could have done without marrying him; but then again, I wouldn't be here, would I?

CHAPTER 5

Life after Dad

"Do not remember the sins of my youth, nor my transgressions; according to your mercy remember me, for your goodness' sake, O LORD."
- Psalm 25:7

Back in Milwaukee, I was going to church and being faithful to God. Now that Dad was dead and gone, he could have no more influence over me, right? Wrong. Linda, the girl who had taken care of Dad, attended the same church our family attended. She dropped by our home one day and said that she was there to see me.

"You made your dad a promise that you would marry me," she reminded me.

"Oh, my dad was dying. I didn't mean anything by that," I told her. "I just said that to get him off my back."

"With your background, you know you're supposed to keep your promises," she warned.

I was only seventeen years old and I wasn't interested in getting married, especially to Linda. Why would I marry someone that I wasn't even attracted to?

This girl started showing up everywhere I went. She stopped by our house and she attended church every time I was there. If I went to the store, she was there. This girl was persistent. She pestered me until she wore me down. I never thought I would do something like this, but at the age of seventeen, I agreed to marry her. I didn't do it because I wanted to; I married her because I thought I was supposed to. I had no clue what I was doing.

The very first week of our marriage, I caught her working on the streets as a prostitute. She even asked me to be her pimp so we could make more money.

What is wrong with this picture? I'm saved, sanctified, and filled with the Holy Spirit, but married to a prostitute who wants me to be her pimp! That was another setup from hell. Friends said this marriage was my dad's final attempt to control me from the grave.

Indeed, Dad's last great act before he died was an act of control. And I was so young and naïve that I fell for it. I made a vow to marry a girl I barely knew. Of course I was not obligated to marry her, but at my age and with my background, I was not thinking too clearly. The enemy used my dad and another evil woman in an attempt to keep me from fulfilling my destiny in Christ.

I now had a wife who was seen regularly with other men. I had no idea where she was from one moment to the next. She tried three times to have me killed, and the fourth time she tried to kill me herself. Then one day she took all the money out of our bank account, left home, and moved in with another man.

Still, I tried against all hope to stay married because I thought that is what I was supposed to do. I thought I was stuck with this woman, and the marriage was going to have to work. To me, divorce was never an option.

My pastor finally said to me, "You don't have to stay with a woman who is committing adultery, living with another man, and trying to have you killed every other week. And if she doesn't kill you with a gun, she's going to kill you with a disease. You are biblically free to divorce this woman."

Four years and two children later, I hired a lawyer and divorced her.

During this time, I developed cancer in my sinus cavities and was receiving radiation treatment. I was on several experimental medications, but doctors had given up hope for my recovery and said that I had six months to live. But my pastor kept praying for me and telling me that God didn't bring me through all of this only to let me die with cancer. He prayed and believed for my healing, and God completely healed me of that cancer.

After the divorce, my pastor's wife came to me with a word: "God said to tell you that you are free, and He has a special lady waiting for you. She described this woman's features to me and said, "She will love you and only you." Then my pastor's wife told me about a youth convention in Miami, Florida. She said, "God told me that you must attend this convention."

I had no money to attend this convention. But my pastor's wife said, "Let's pray and ask God to make a way."

Not long after that, I received a phone call from an older cousin of mine that we had lived with when we first moved to Milwaukee. He heard that I wanted to attend a youth convention but had no money.

"How much money do you need?" he asked.

"I need four hundred dollars."

"I'll be right there." Sure enough, here he came with four hundred dollars.

God answered prayer, and soon I was on my way to a youth convention in Miami. It was one of the best moves I ever made because that is where I met a young woman named Selena. I had just checked into this fancy hotel and decided to step outside and see the sights. I walked to the front door and looked out. Standing outside the hotel was a young woman who was as beautiful to me as the sun that was shining in the

Florida sky. She looked like the girl of my dreams, and she looked just like the woman that my pastor's wife described to me.

But she was standing next to a man that I assumed was her husband. Later I learned that he was a deacon in her church. I saw her throughout the convention, and we smiled at each other every time we passed. But I never got up enough nerve to actually speak or introduce myself.

Then one day the convention sponsored a concert and my friend Bill and I arrived late. When we got there, the room was filled with young people from around the world. Except for two seats close to the front, there were no seats left in the room. The usher seated us in those two seats.

As we sat down, a young lady in front of me turned around and said, "So what is your name?" My jaw dropped. It was the friend of the beautiful young lady I had been eyeing throughout the entire convention.

I could barely speak, but I managed to say, "My name is Curtis."

Then, in front of perhaps a thousand people, she introduced me to the beautiful young lady. "Well, Curtis, this is Selena. Everybody, this is Curtis." The entire room clapped. I was sure my friend Bill was behind it all.

After the concert, Selena and I talked. We were together for the rest of the convention. I thought it best to tell her my life story right up front, so I did. I told her about my father, my background, my life of practicing voodoo, the woman I married and divorced, and my two children. I thought for sure that after she heard about my past I would never see her again.

Instead, we fell in love. She lived in Baltimore, Maryland and I lived in Milwaukee, Wisconsin so we exchanged phone numbers. We talked on the phone every day. Finally I decided to go to Baltimore and ask her parents for her hand in marriage.

I bought a plane ticket and headed for Baltimore. On the way, the airplane developed trouble as we were flying over Lansing, Michigan. Sparks were coming from one of the airplane wings and we were falling like a ride on a roller coaster. People were panicking and the cabin was in chaos. The pilot's voice came across the intercom and said, "We are going to do an emergency landing in a cornfield in Lansing. Please remain in your seats and put your head between your knees."

We were still heading down like a roller coaster when I heard the voice of God say to me, "Do not fear. You will live and not die."

Suddenly it felt as though a hand reached under the plane and pulled us back up from the sudden drop. The pilot didn't understand what happened, but we were able to make it to Detroit where we landed safely.

The plane was checked and they decided to let the flight continue to Baltimore. Only two passengers got back on the plane—me and one other person. Nothing was going to keep me from getting to Baltimore to ask for Selena's hand in marriage.

The plane continued the flight to Baltimore with no problems. Selena was at the airport to pick me up and drive me to her parents' home. I told them all about my past; I held nothing back. I told them about my life before Jesus and my life after I became a new creation in Christ. They gave me permission to marry Selena, and they gave us their blessings.

Selena worked for the Federal Bureau of Investigation, so they had to check my background to make sure that she could marry me and still remain employed with the FBI. I am thankful to say that they approved me, and Selena was allowed to keep her job.

When Selena's pastor learned that she was engaged to me, he was furious. He had already chosen Selena as a wife for his own son, and he tried to talk her out of marrying me. He told her, "This guy is a thug and I forbid you to marry him. I want you to marry my son."

Selena ignored him. But for several years after we married, her former pastor sent me hateful messages. One day I'd had enough. I called him and said, "I have been nothing but a gentleman to you, but you keep throwing my past in my face. If I hear that you have said so much as one word about me, I will come to Baltimore and beat you within an inch of your life. If you know my past as you say you do, then you know I'm capable of doing it."

The next time we were in Baltimore visiting Selena's parents, her pastor called and invited us to dinner. He took us to the fanciest restaurant in town and paid for our dinner. I forgave him and asked him to forgive me for threatening to kill him. He and I became friends and remained so until he died.

In October of 1980, before Selena and I were married, I moved to California. When I was a child, Dad took us to California for a visit. I loved the state, with all the warm weather, sunshine, and fruit trees. "I'll live in this state someday," I said to myself. I saw my upcoming marriage as my opportunity to move to California and make a new start.

When I arrived in California I lived briefly with my sister, but I knew that the Lord was leading me to the Los Angeles area. I left my sister's home and moved to Los Angeles where I lived with a friend of mine, Pastor Shumate and his wife. After living with them for a short time, they offered to let me move into a house they owned in the Watts area of South Central Los Angeles.

If you recall the Watts riots of 1965 or the Rodney King riots of 1992, you will know that Watts is one of the roughest areas of Los Angeles. But having been raised in a rough area of Connecticut, I figured I could handle it.

I drove to look at this house on Zamora Avenue, situated right in the heart of Watts, and found gang members gambling on the front porch.

I quickly learned that the house had been used as a brothel by the previous residents. They kept a log of just about everything that happened by writing it on the walls. They had written things such as, "So and so got pregnant in this spot on this date."

The house was full of rats, and the water bugs were the size of my thumb. I killed seventeen mice and rats the first week, and about that many water bugs in one night. The walls looked as though they had been painted with soot from the fireplace. I cleared so much trash out of the house that it filled about a hundred garbage bags. On trash collection day, I watched the garbage collectors shake their heads in disbelief at all the garbage piled in front of the house.

One of the bathroom sinks was so clogged up from years of neglect that nothing would unstop it. I rigged a mechanism in which a pipe ran from underneath the sink, and I connected it so that it drained into the toilet. When the sink was used, the water ran into the toilet instead of down the drain.

The roof of the house didn't just leak; it flooded. When it rained, you could take a shower in the living room. The furnace was broken and the back of the house was cold in the wintertime. I improvised again. I hung a fan on the ceiling, turned on the stove, and turned on the fan so that it would pull warm air into the back of the house.

I slept at Pastor Shumate's house at night and, during the day, I cleaned, painted, and repaired this house in Watts the best I could. I worked from morning until almost midnight. After I fixed the place up, Pastor Shumate told me that I could have the house.

Selena and I were married on November 21, 1981. We moved into the house in Watts, along with my two children who had been staying at the Shumate home. Selena immediately started putting the woman's touch on the place. And since the house had been used as a brothel, we had to do some serious spiritual warfare after we moved in. The place was full of demonic spirits from all the sinful activity of the previous residents.

We had almost no personal belongings. The people who moved out of the house left a beat-up sleep sofa behind. One arm of the sofa was gone and the back was missing. We used this as a bed. We had to lie down very slowly or the metal frame would cut us. After cutting myself badly on that metal frame, I heard the Lord say, "This too shall pass." My father-in-law came to visit and saw where we were sleeping. He helped us get a bed.

We could not afford new furnishings for the house, so over the years, we filled it with things that other people had thrown away. My son Scott and I would drive down the road and find things people had discarded. I would stop the car and tell Scott to get out and load up the item.

"Oh, Dad, that's embarrassing," he always said. "Somebody might see me."

Still he jumped out and threw the item in the back of the station wagon. We took the things home, fixed them up, and let somebody in the house use them. As Scott grew older and we no longer collected other peoples' throwaways, he still talked about how we used to pick up other people's junk from the sidewalks.

After moving to California, Selena continued to work with the FBI. Since I had always been a good fighter and had previous boxing experience, I decided to try boxing. I began training, and my first fight was in 1982. I was hoping for a shot at the Olympics. And even though I was on the roster, at the last minute they replaced me with Tyrell Biggs. Still, Don King was impressed with my boxing ability, and he and Joe Jackson wanted to get me involved in professional boxing. The two of them agreed that they would become my co-managers.

I was thrilled about the prospect of getting involved in professional boxing. Then one bright summer day I was driving to pick Selena up from work when a car that was driven by an eighty-nine-year-old woman crossed the yellow line and hit me head on at a speed of about fifty miles an hour. The front wheels of both our cars lifted off the ground, and she slammed me into three other cars. The seat belt that I was wearing cut into my neck and caused a terrible neck injury. According to my doctors, the injury led to a cancerous tumor.

I was attending West Adams Foursquare Church at that time. Juanita Smith was a great deliverance minister, so she and other pastors of that church laid hands on me and prayed. They said that as they prayed, they felt something come off my neck and run down the aisle of the church. When the doctor performed surgery on my neck, he removed a lump the size of a lemon. But when they performed the biopsy, there was no cancer.

That accident destroyed my dream of professional boxing, at least for the time being. Don King and Joe Jackson moved on with Mike Tyson and other fighters.

But ten years later, I felt well enough to try boxing again. I traveled to Las Vegas and talked to Don King personally. He encouraged me to try again, and he and Joe Jackson became my co-managers. I fought as a professional boxer from 1996 until 2001.

At that time I weighed two hundred fifty-five pounds, which qualified me for the heavyweight class. I am six foot five with a body like a steel wall. The palm of my hand is at least twice the size of an average person's palm, so I can throw a hard punch. King and Jackson were selective about the people they let me fight.

Throwing a hard punch should be an advantage in boxing, but it actually kept me from getting some of the fights I wanted. I told King that

I wanted to spar with Mike Tyson and George Foreman, but he told me that I punched too hard. Mike refused to fight me, even though it would have been a six million dollar fight. I asked George if he would give me a fight and he replied, "Look at those hands of yours. There is no way I'm going to fight you."

One time I had a sparring match with a champion boxer, and I punched his shoulder so hard that it fractured his ankle. He still tells me that I am incapable of hitting somebody without hurting them.

When I trained at the gym, the walls would sometimes shake. During my boxing career, when I hit somebody with an uppercut, you could almost feel the punch as you watched it on television. There have been times when I had to stop and apologize for hitting somebody so hard. I have a pleasant demeanor, but my wife and family feel very safe when I'm around.

Once I was in a boxing match that wasn't going well for me. I decided to take my chances and throw a straight punch as I closed my eyes. When I did, I hit my opponent—a fighter who is the current champion in California—so hard that he fell to the floor and didn't get back up. The sports announcer shouted, "He's like an earthquake!" And that is how I got the nickname Earthquake Kelley, which has stuck to this day.

The last man I boxed was James "Hellfire" Harris. I watched his video over and over, and I knew I could beat this guy. I was favored to win. And on the day of the fight, people packed out the room at the Irvine Marriott Hotel.

I was so eager to get in the ring and win that fight that I started saying to myself, "I'm going to kill this guy. When I get in the ring, I'm going to destroy this guy."

But I heard the voice of God rebuke me and say, "If you don't get that spirit of murder off you, I'm not going to let you win this fight."

The Lord kept rebuking and warning me as the thought kept coming to mind, "I'm going to kill this guy."

Before the fight the referee came into the room to check on me. He took one look at me and said, "Earthquake, you don't look so good."

"I'm fine," I replied.

"I'm going to take your blood pressure anyway."

When he checked it, his eyes reflected shock as he said, "Earthquake, are you still alive? How did your blood pressure get so high? What have you done to make your blood pressure go up like this?"

"I didn't do anything. I'm just sitting here getting ready to fight."

The referee was so concerned that he brought in the doctor. He re-checked my blood pressure and said, "Earthquake, something is wrong with you. There is no way you can go in that ring and fight. We are going to stop this fight tonight."

"I have to fight," I replied. "There's a crowd of people out there who are here to see me fight."

They insisted on stopping the fight, but I told them that people were there to see me fight, and I was going in the ring to fight anyway. I still had the desire to destroy my opponent, and God continued to warn me that if I went into the ring with that attitude, I was on my own. He was not going into the ring with me.

"If you go into that ring and fight, we're taking away your license," the officials warned me.

I disobeyed their orders not to fight and went into the ring anyway. As I stepped into the room, the crowd shouted, "Earthquake! Earthquake!" I was pumped up and just knew I was going to win that fight.

Suddenly I began to lose my vision and my left hand froze. I heard the voice of God say, "It's not too late to repent."

I'm ashamed to say that I actually told God, "No, he's as good as dead."

Hellfire Harris and I entered the ring. I was doing okay in the first round. One of my boxing techniques was to corner my opponent and hit until he gave up. I cut Harris off in the corner and battered him with everything I had. He was just about to drop when a dark cloud came over me and I lost my sight completely. He saw that I was letting up and a second wind hit him; he battered me as I fell backwards against the ropes. I had never been counted out in a fight. But Hellfire Harris, a man that I should have easily beaten, won the fight that night.

God spoke to me and said, "Son, you refused to listen to my voice. If you had listened to me, none of this would have happened. I did not give you power to fight so that you could kill."

I had a stroke that night, and I lost my license to fight for disobeying orders not to fight. When I lost that fight, I lost credibility. Sure, I could punch, but what good was that when I was rebellious? If you looked up the word rebellion in the dictionary, my picture should have been next to it.

People accused me of taking a bribe to throw the fight that night. I had been favored to win, so it was totally unexpected that I would go down in the first round. But no bribery was involved; it was God Himself who took me out.

Perhaps it was to my benefit that I never had another fight because boxing is a barbaric sport. Statistically, eighty-seven percent of boxers will suffer a brain injury during their career. One day I thought to myself, "I wonder what happened to Greg Page?" Greg was a great heavyweight boxer who kept coming back for another fight. One evening I was flipping through the television channels when I saw Greg on a medical channel. The story told how that he decided to become active in professional boxing again at age forty-two. Greg fought a young, left-handed boxer and was holding his own until the tenth round. Greg had expected his opponent's punch to come from one direction; but instead, it came from the other. His opponent hit a straight left flush to Page's chin and knocked him unconscious. The blow separated his brain from his skull and caused a serious brain injury that resulted in a massive stroke. Today he is paralyzed on the left side and confined to a wheelchair.

I almost cried when I saw what had happened to Greg. I told Selena, "You know, that could have been me."

Before my career ended, I had a dream one night that I was boxing George Foreman and had him cornered. I caught him in an overhand right jab and, in the dream, George died. I dreamed that people all over the world hated me. Can you imagine living the rest of your life as the man who killed George Foreman? He is a good Christian man, and he used to be my prayer partner. I would never want to see anything bad happen to him.

I knew a fifteen-year old boy in Los Angeles named David that I tried to talk out of boxing. I said, "David, you're a young, nice-looking guy. You're a great comedian. Maybe you should get a good job and try to get into acting. Boxing is a rough sport and you can get hurt very easily."

"I can do it," he kept telling me.

"Look," I told him. "There are some rough characters in boxing. Some of them might put you in a ring prematurely and you can get hurt badly. There are punches coming at you that are like hammers hitting you."

But he was determined to fight. I didn't have a good feeling about him boxing. Two days after our conversation, somebody came to me and said, "Did you hear about David? He got into a sparring match at the gym and got hit hard. He went home, sat on the porch, and fell over dead."

David was a great young man and I loved him like my own son. I hated to see that happen to him. More than likely, somebody at the gym put him in a sparring match with a fighter who was too seasoned for him. And in the match, he received a deadly head injury.

Only God knows what might have happened had I continued boxing. I cannot look back and complain that my career ended as it did. Besides, God has plans to use that fight. He has recently instructed me to use the video of that fight as an example of what happens to people who are in rebellion. God is serious about the sin of rebellion.

During my boxing career, I worked various jobs to supplement our income. I also began a drug treatment center ministry called The BRIDGE. This was an acronym for "in Him we live and move and have our Being; Righteousness; Instruction; Deliverance; Guidance; and Eternity. People came to this center for drug counseling and prayer. We started The BRIDGE in 1985 in Carson, California on a street called Grace, and we worked under the ministry of Pastors Marvin and Juanita Smith at the West Adams Foursquare Church. The Smiths were deliverance ministers who allowed me the freedom to preach true deliverance.

We were renting a building in Carson and things were going well. But the pastors asked us to move into their church facility to minister to the people they couldn't handle. In exchange, they gave us free rent. We moved there in 1986 and started a ministry with three people in attendance. It grew quickly and people to whom we were ministering brought their children. That led us to start The BRIDGE Kidz. Those children brought their friends, and the ministry kept growing. Soon we had packed facilities two nights a week. The people that God delivered through The BRIDGE have gone on to become choir members, deacons, elders, and preachers. They are affecting the whole city of Los Angeles, California and some are preaching around the world.

From there, the ministry kept growing. But the pastor developed cancer and died, and another minister took over the church. When he came on board, he fired me because he said I was starting a church within a church. He wanted to start his own organization with his own people. When that didn't last, he tried to hire me back but I chose not to return.

Both Selena and I had a vision to see people come to the Lord. She had a vision for runaway children, and I had a vision to see people delivered from drug addiction and witchcraft. So we started a church in our home. Often we had a packed house, and sometimes people didn't want to leave. Some came on Tuesday night and stayed until Sunday.

From the beginning of our marriage, we invited people into our home when they needed help. The first person who stayed with us was a friend of Selena's who had lived in Baltimore and was going through a divorce. Then we took in an actress. Little by little, we started bringing people into our home to help them get delivered and back on their feet. The word spread and, at one time, we had so many people in our home that the only places not being used for guests were the master bedroom and the bathtub.

We also wanted to feed the poor, so I asked local companies to donate food and other items. Being well-known in the area as a boxer, I could introduce myself as Earthquake Kelley and get an immediate open door. Companies started giving us food, shoes, coats, backpacks for children, detergents, and toiletry items. One year someone donated so many turkeys that we were able to go door to door in Watts and hand out the food. Over the years, we developed a tremendous network of organizations that gave us items to help the poor.

Throughout Hollywood, well-known people learned that there was a place in Watts where you could get clean from drugs or get your life straightened up. We housed people from all walks of life—gang members from the Crips and the Bloods, drug addicts, the daughter of a man heavily involved in the pornography industry, politicians, sports figures, actors, and other people who worked in the film industry.

We rescued people from the streets of Hollywood. In one instance, we rescued a young girl named Jessica that I heard about from the gym where I boxed. She had no money to support herself, so she had been sleeping with the owner of the gym to have money to live. I told her to pack her things and move into our house.

Our children—Scott, Zina, Angela, Keme, Christopher, Cherish, and Curtis, Jr.—never knew what it was like to live in a house without other people living with us. We constantly had people in our home that we ministered to and helped get back on their feet. It didn't matter to the people we helped that we lived in Watts. They came to our home anyway, and we protected them. Not even the people in our neighborhood knew who we were housing.

Over the years, we gained a lot of respect throughout the Los Angeles area for our ministry. People knew they would be in good hands while in our home. But on December 7, 1998 an incident occurred that would change our lives forever.

CHAPTER 6

Death and Rebellion

"Not everyone who says to me, 'Lord, Lord,' shall enter the kingdom of heaven, but he who does the will of my Father in heaven."
- Matthew 7:21

I was at a ministers' convention in Las Vegas on December 7 and had tried to reach several family members on their cell phones—Selena, Scott, Zina, and others—but nobody answered their phone. I knew that something must be wrong.

When I went back to the hotel I received a call from Selena. She said, "Baby, I have the worst news. A guy carjacked Scott and Curtis, Jr."

"What happened?" I asked.

"He shot and killed Scott."

In that moment, my world fell apart. I could not believe my son was dead, killed by a carjacker. I screamed, I cried, and I hit the walls. God let me rave for a while before He spoke to me audibly and said, "Son, I didn't do this. Don't hold anything in your heart against me. I want you to forgive. I want you to preach forgiveness and love. Something great will come out of this."

God asked me, "What does a Christian parent want for their children? What do they want besides a good marriage and a good job?"

I replied, "For their children to make it into heaven."

"Your son is with me," God said. "I know what you are feeling. My Son died, too, and I had to watch it. You don't see it now, but many people are going to be blessed. On the other side of your tears, you will see it."

I left immediately to return to Los Angeles. There were no seats left on the plane, but they gave me a seat that was assigned to a flight attendant. I got off the plane and there was Selena, waiting for me and crying. Except for Curtis, Jr. who was nowhere to be found, all of the family was at the house when I arrived. Our lives were in a tailspin.

The day before he was killed, Scott and I were in the kitchen pretending to box each other. Suddenly he stopped and a serious look came across his face. He grabbed me, hugged me tightly, and said, "I love you, Dad. I'm so proud of you and Mom. Promise me that if anything happens, you and Mom will not stop preaching deliverance. Promise me that you will never stop helping people."

I couldn't understand why he suddenly had become so serious and was hugging me so tightly. I asked him, "What's wrong, son? Did something happen on your job? Did somebody hurt your feelings?"

"No, Dad, nothing like that. Promise me that you and Mom will never stop helping people and preaching deliverance no matter what people say or do. Promise me or I'm not going to stop hugging you."

When I promised him that I would never stop preaching deliverance, Scott left the kitchen crying.

Scott was about eleven years old in 1985 when he came to live with us. His birth mother placed him in my charge, and we took him into our home and raised him as our own child. He was with me every day of the week, and I was the only father he ever knew. He and I were very close. Scott was twenty-four years old when he died; never would I have imagined that December 7, 1998 would be Scott's last day on earth.

My cousin owned the morgue where Scott's body was being kept, and I went to the morgue and prayed for him to come back to life. Scott died with a smile on his face, and it almost seemed that he was saying, "No, Dad. I'm staying right where I am."

I preached Scott's funeral, even though people advised me not to. I was sure I could be strong enough to get through the service, but I was not. I lost it halfway through. Two other ministers were there, and they finished the service for me. The church was packed with standing room only. People commented that they were not aware that Scott knew all of those people.

Scott's killer was the cousin of a family we had been feeding. They lived a short distance down the street from our home, and we gave them so much food that they should have been dependents on our tax return. The father was a drug addict and we spent many hours ministering to him. The attacker knew exactly who he was shooting. It was no secret that Scott and Curtis were my sons; everybody in Watts knew it.

This man had approached Scott and Curtis and demanded their car just as they were getting into it. My sons recognized the guy, so they ignored his demand and got into the car. Scott sat behind the wheel and Curtis, Jr. on the passenger's side.

But the guy was determined to take the car. He pulled a gun and pointed it at Scott. The last words Scott spoke before the man shot him were, "Hey man, I'm the Bishop's son!" The assailant pulled Scott's body into the street and jumped in the car beside Curtis. He tried to shoot Curtis, but he was able to wrestle the gun from the attacker and shoot him in the arm. The attacker jumped out of the car and over Scott's dead body and ran. When he showed up at the hospital to have his gunshot wound treated, the police arrested him.

For six months, we went to court and listened to this case. We watched as the court showed pictures, day after day, of Scott's dead and bleeding body on the ground. Those six months were grueling for our family. The man who killed Scott was sentenced to four life sentences for carjacking, murder, and attempted murder.

People don't realize who they are affecting by being a gangster. They don't realize how many people are hurt by their actions. The parents, brothers and sisters, aunts and uncles, and many friends are robbed when a gangster takes the life of another person. I kept expecting to hear Scott's footsteps coming down the hall. Selena cried every day for a year. Our youngest daughter kept asking, "Where's Scott?" All of the children were affected by Scott's death; especially Curtis, Jr., who saw him being killed.

I thank God that I was no longer living with my old mindset when Scott was killed. With my voodoo background, I could have become enraged and sent curses to kill the entire family. I could have used my knowledge of voodoo to get revenge. The old Curtis would have destroyed the whole family, but God told me right up front that I had to forgive and teach others to forgive. He told me that the enemy would continue to bring this up, and He warned me not to let it defeat me. He told me to keep loving people and preaching salvation, forgiveness, and deliverance.

Forgiveness does not mean that a parent stops missing and thinking about their deceased child. I miss Scott every day of my life, and it is still hard for me to tell this story. Scott helped me in the ministry and attended conferences with me. Every summer we participated in a fishing tournament. I can't do any of those things with him anymore. He wrote music and organized a Christian hip-hop group that disbanded after he died. It is such a tragedy when a young person with so much potential is suddenly taken from you.

We continued to help people, but my heart was no longer in it. Since we lived in Watts and the man who killed our son also lived in Watts, it seemed that we were helping the very people who killed our son. I lost my thirst to help them. I thought, "What's the use? Why bother?"

God kept reminding me that not everybody in Watts killed our son. Still, I let his death eat away at my soul until I developed an attitude that I didn't care if everybody in Watts went straight to hell. I had been faithful to these people for years, and the only thing I had to show for it was a dead son.

Gang members asked for our help and I refused. "But you've always helped us," they said. "You've been like a father to us."

But I didn't care. Every time I saw a gang member who was killed by police, I thought, "Good. That's what you get." When I saw that something terrible happened to their families, I thought, "Good. You're getting what you deserve." I didn't care if they all died.

We stayed in Watts for three years after Scott was killed. Not only did I have to deal with my feelings toward the people in Watts, I also had to deal with three ministers who were persecuting me for preaching deliverance. When I preached, the altars were filled with people who got delivered by the power of the Holy Spirit. People fell under the power of God and received healing from bondages that had plagued them for years. Still, these three well-known preachers tried to destroy my family, my reputation, and my ministry.

These men told me and others, "It doesn't take all of that. Deliverance is outdated. Deliverance died when Jesus died. Just preach the Golden Rule."

One minister said, "Earthquake, you take this salvation thing too seriously. You are *too* saved. Lighten up."

Another minister suggested, "We need to have you hypnotized so we can see if you're telling the truth."

I was even asked, "How many girlfriends do you have?"

"None," I replied. "I have a wife."

The minister replied, "I have a wife *and* a girlfriend."

I found out that some of these men were in serious need of deliverance themselves, and that is why they didn't want to hear a message of deliverance.

This persecution had been going on since I started preaching deliverance. From the very beginning of my ministry, I taught people that they could fight off anything the devil threw at them. Even after Scott's death, and even though I was battling my own feelings of despair, I never stopped believing that God could deliver us out of any situation. But it was not a popular message with some ministers.

Perhaps it was the added stress of losing Scott that caused these ministers to finally wear me down. I said, "Lord, I don't understand this. I'm faithful to you. Why don't you make these guys back down?"

God said, "Ignore them and preach deliverance anyway."

But instead of obeying God, I gave up and let the enemy win that battle. I said to God, "I will never, ever preach deliverance again. I quit."

Since I no longer wanted to help the people in Watts, and since I was determined to no longer preach deliverance, I decided to run as far away from Southern California as I could get. So in October of 2001, I loaded up our belongings and moved my family to a house in the mountains of Woodstock, New York. We arrived, but the truck with our belongings did not. To this day we have never seen one item that the mover was supposed to have transported to New York from California.

When we moved, I purposely did not give any forwarding address. I was so upset that I didn't want anybody to know where we were. I didn't want anybody to call, write, or visit. I wanted to hibernate in my own little corner of the world and not deal with another person outside of my immediate family.

The first week that we were in Woodstock, I received a letter in the mail. It had no return address on the envelope, but it was sent from Costa Mesa, California. Inside the envelope was a booklet entitled, "Repent from your sins and decree a thing."

"Repent of what?" I said. "I don't drink, I don't chew, and I don't run with those who do. I'm not chasing another man's wife or his brother. So what do I have to repent of?" I ripped up the booklet.

Selena said, "Babe, don't rip that up. There are scriptures in there!"

"I don't care," was my response.

Right away, I received a telephone call. Since we had an unlisted phone number, nobody could have gotten the number to call me. Nobody even knew where we were. The person on the other end of the line was someone I knew from Seattle, Washington. He said, "You are out of God's will; you need to repent."

Fifteen minutes later, somebody in Long Beach, California called to tell me the same thing: repent. That day, seven people from different parts of the country called and told me to repent because I was out of the will of God. When I asked how they got my phone number, they replied, "Never mind how I got your number. God told me to call you and tell you to repent." None of these people who called even knew each other. But in one day's time, they all called and told me that I needed to repent because I was out of God's will.

I was so mad when I went to bed that night that you could have fried an egg on my head. Selena was beside me sleeping like a baby. As I lay in bed, I looked up at the ceiling and saw the big face spirit—the same one that had tormented me as a child. This evil spirit was laughing at me as it said, "Mr. Deliverance, huh?"

I said, "Get out of here, in the name of Jesus."

"I'm not leaving."

"Get out of my house!"

"You can't make me leave. You can't make me do anything. You have no power over me because you are in rebellion. You are no better than I am," the spirit replied with laughter.

That demonic spirit would not leave. It stayed in the room and taunted me until I heard the sound of marching in the house. My first thought was that somebody had broken into the house, but it sounded more like a small army. I realized I didn't have any way to defend myself from that many people, so I decided to lie in bed and pretend I was asleep. When they got to the bedroom, I planned to take out the biggest one first, and then worry about the smaller ones.

The footsteps came into the bedroom, and I was peeking through half-closed eyelids while still hoping they would think I was asleep. I felt something nudging the bed as though they were trying to wake me up. Then I heard a voice say, "Open your eyes."

When I opened my eyes, there were seven men around my bed—three on each side and one at the foot. The six men on the sides were standing at attention. The one at the foot of the bed spoke and said, "You are stiff-necked, rebellious, and hard-hearted. You let a handful of so-called ministers stop you from doing what God called you to do. Repent! Go back to California and finish the work God told you to do."

This man seemed to be very upset with me. I was sure I must be dreaming. I opened and closed my eyes several times, trying to figure out whether I was awake or asleep. Each time I opened my eyes, the men were still around the bed. I realized I was indeed wide awake.

The man at the foot of the bed spoke again. "God has done so much for you. Do you remember when he spared you from the snapping turtle? Do you remember all the people who tried to shoot you? Do you remember when the gang member tried to cut your throat? Do you remember when you died of a drug overdose? God spared your life many times. He even brought you back from hell. God has much invested in you. You have knowledge that can help people. Repent now of your disobedience. Go back to California and preach deliverance like God told you to do. This is your last warning. If you do not repent and obey, the next angel you receive will be the death angel. Take this seriously."

By this time it was obvious that God had sent an army of angels to deliver a message to me. After the angel spoke, I watched as all seven of them rose into the air and disappeared through the ceiling of our bedroom. I jumped out of bed and woke Selena. I told her about the men in the bedroom who were not really men because they left through the ceiling. I relayed the message they brought to me.

The day after this angelic visitation, we drove the twenty miles to Wal-Mart. On the way back, we saw beautiful multi-colored lights dancing around the inside of our car. I thought perhaps they were police flashers, so I told Selena to pull over. She did, and we waited about ten minutes and never saw a police car. As we watched these lights dance around the interior of the car, I heard a voice say, "Take this seriously. This is very serious." I realized these lights were a sign from God, who was telling me to go back to California and be obedient to what He called me to do.

But I still did not return right away. God kept telling me, "Go back to California. I have a building prepared for you in Hollywood." There was no doubt in my mind that I was supposed to go back to California. I continued to receive confirmation of that. On one occasion, I went to a church in Tuscaloosa, Alabama with a friend. Before I could sit down, the minister pointed to me and said, "Don't sit down yet. The Lord has a word for you. He said to tell you that you are in New York and you're supposed to be in California and you know it. God has a place for you. Go to California and stop running from God. Go home and pack."

It was 2003 before I finally moved the family back to California. But I did not go to Hollywood like God instructed. I argued with Him and said, "God, I can't go to Hollywood. I don't have a building in Hollywood." Instead of obeying the Lord and trusting that He had a building for us in Hollywood, I joined the staff of a church that was about sixty miles from Hollywood. My wife took a job as a secretary at this same church. I reasoned that since I was back in California and working in a church, surely I must be in the will of God. Instead of trusting and obeying, I took the easy way out.

We did not want to move back into the house that we still owned in the Watts area of Los Angeles because it held too many bad memories. So we moved into a house about sixty miles from Hollywood in the mountains of Littlerock, California.

We stayed at this church for two years, but I could hear the Spirit of God saying, "I told you to go to Hollywood, but you're still being disobedient." Finally God said, "This is your last warning. Now I'm sending the death angel."

One Wednesday night after church I developed the worst headache of my life. My vision became blurry, my hearing became dull, and my head felt like somebody had poured boiling water over it. I was losing consciousness. I thought perhaps it was an old injury from my boxing career, so I didn't go to the hospital right away. After suffering with this for two days, Selena drove me to the hospital where I was diagnosed with a brain aneurysm. The doctor told me that most people who have a brain aneurysm die within two hours after the blood vessel bursts, so it was a miracle that I was still living.

They admitted me to the hospital immediately. As I lay on the bed in agonizing pain, God spoke to me and said, "I told you to take this seriously. I told you to go to Hollywood and preach deliverance but you let a handful of so-called ministers stop you. Now I am going to show you what happens to people who die in rebellion."

At that moment the medical staff gave me a shot of morphine, which felt like hot lava running through my veins. It seemed as though an elephant was standing on my chest and I could no longer breathe. I tried to hold onto the sides of the hospital bed as I began to convulse. The walls of the room appeared to turn upside down and it seemed that I was falling off the side of a building. Then my heart stopped. Immediately I felt myself falling backwards at a fast rate of speed. When I realized that I was falling into hell I thought, "I'm going in the wrong direction! I'm supposed to be going up!"

The closer I came to hell, the more I could hear people screaming, "Help me! Help! Don't do that to me! Somebody get me out of here! Jesus, forgive me! Give me another chance! I'll do what you told me to do!"

It dawned on me that I was listening to people who had been told to do something by God and they didn't do it. I was listening to disobedient people who died in their rebellion. And I was getting ready to join them.

When I fell within a foot of the hands of evil spirits that were reaching toward me, other hands beneath me grabbed me and pulled me back up. I heard the voice of God say, "I wanted you to see what happens to rebellious people who refuse to do what I tell them to do. Rebellion is as the sin of witchcraft. Not one rebellious person will enter into my kingdom."

I came back into my body and heard my wife and the doctor shouting my name, "Curtis! Curtis!" The heart monitor had flat lined and they were working swiftly to bring me back to life. Then I heard one of the doctors say, "We lost him."

I wanted to tell them I wasn't dead, but I could not speak. It seemed that I was stuck between life and death. Then I heard God say, "Open your eyes." When I did, the doctor said, "You're back! We thought we had lost you!"

They stabilized me and placed me in intensive care where they watched me around the clock. The doctor concluded that an allergic reaction to morphine had stopped my heart. Still, several times over the next few days, a nurse tried to give me morphine. Thankfully there were other nurses in the unit who said, "No, you can't give him morphine. It almost killed him earlier."

Thank God I was alive, but I still was not out of danger. I felt like twenty men were beating my temple and the top of my head with lead pipes. It seemed that my head was roasting in a hot oven, and I had three blocks of ice on each side of my head at all times. My throat had nearly closed and I often choked on the food they tried to feed me. The medical staff had a difficult time bringing down my blood pressure, which was so high at times that the doctors questioned why I was still alive. I could barely move a muscle, so it seemed that I was strapped in a prison hospital bed.

I had some wonderful nurses and doctors, but there was one nurse that I'm certain was sent straight from hell to kill me. Each time she entered the room, I felt a demonic presence come with her. I was even afraid to touch the food she brought to my room. One time I almost fell out of the bed and this nurse sneered, "I'm sick of you!" as she gave me a shoulder punch and pushed me back into the bed with the force of a linebacker. My ribs hurt for hours afterward.

I was connected to oxygen because I could barely breathe without it, but this nurse came into my room one night and intentionally disconnected my oxygen. It was a miracle that I survived because my oxygen was not reconnected until the doctor came to visit the next morning. He was furious as he yelled, "Who unplugged Mr. Kelley's oxygen? Don't you know he will die without oxygen?"

Not long after that I had another unusual experience. A different nurse was in my room one day when two strange visitors entered the room. I thought it was odd that she failed to acknowledge them and even walked right past them as though they were invisible. One of the men sat in a chair near the foot of my bed while the other stood and looked at me. The one who sat in the chair raised his middle finger at me and mumbled words that I recognized as witchcraft curses. He had a look of disgust on his face, and I immediately realized that these men were not brothers in Christ who had come to visit and pray with me.

Then I noticed the men were not wearing shirts. I wondered how they got past the nurses' station without shirts. One of the men also had an extra large head and the thought occurred to me that he must have an enormous brain tumor.

As these thoughts were going through my mind, the man sitting in the chair spoke. "We have been trying to kill you for years but you just won't die."

"Excuse me?"

Using foul language, one of the men told me, "You're going to die! You're going to die! You will not leave this hospital! You're going to die!"

I could hardly believe what I was hearing. "What did you say?" I managed to mutter, almost daring him to say it again. Being a fighter, my first inclination was to get out of bed and punch both of them, even though I could barely make a fist and had no strength to do more than merely think about it. I thought to myself, "Lord, what is this? Who are these men? Why are they coming to this hospital cursing me?"

I heard the Holy Spirit say, "These are not human beings. They are evil spirits from the kingdom of hell. Their master, the devil, sent them. Throughout your whole life, they have been assigned to kill you. You cannot fight them with your fists; it won't do any good, son. The weapons of your warfare are not carnal, but mighty through God to the pulling down of strongholds. Use the name of Jesus. Plead the blood."

Immediately I said, "In the name of Jesus, leave my room. I plead the blood of Jesus." As soon as they heard the name of Jesus, they shouted, "No!" and disappeared through the floor.

That night I felt the bed move and I heard yelling and obscenities in my ear. I kept pleading the blood of Jesus to get rid of these evil spirits. It was clear to me that I was in the middle of a serious spiritual battle. When I told Selena what happened, she and other believers started interceding for me. She advised me to keep calling on the name of Jesus and not allow the devil to frighten me.

That is what I did. Each time I became fearful, or each time I suffered intense pain, I called on the name of Jesus. His presence came into my room and left peace in my spirit. Just like the Bible says, if you keep your mind on the Lord, He will keep you in perfect peace.

CHAPTER 7

This is Paradise

"So we are always confident, knowing that while we are at home in the body, we are absent from the Lord...we are confident, yes, well pleased rather to be absent from the body and to be present with the Lord."

- 2 Corinthians 5:6,8

One night I asked the nurse to close my door so that I could be alone with God. As I lay in the hospital bed, I started praising God for sparing my life again. You can imagine how thankful I was that He once again rescued me from hell. I thought about how rebellious I had been, about all the time I had wasted, and about the hurt I had caused God. That night I praised Him with everything I had in me. I said, "Thank you, Jesus" as many times as I could. Then I rested my head on my pillow and let the tears flow down my face.

As I rested and cried, I noticed that the room was becoming brighter. It wasn't completely dark in the room because there were street lights outside that were lighting up the room. But this light was not coming from street lights.

I looked around the room to locate the source of the light and saw something descend from the ceiling. I could feel a strong presence of God in the room, and I was in awe as I watched a beautiful rectangular golden box with intricate designs carved on it come through the ceiling and into the room. The box appeared to be covered with flakes of pure gold. As I stared in amazement, it became clear that someone who was a magnificent artist had designed this vessel. I didn't know at the time what this was, but in 2006 I saw a hand-built replica of the Ark of the Covenant. That Ark, without the two cherubim, reminded me of the box that came into my room.

Suddenly I felt as though I had separated from my body. I was light as a feather as I hovered over my body and looked at the guy who was lying in the bed with tubes in his arm and an oxygen cord up his nose. I thought to myself, "That guy is in terrible shape. It doesn't look like he's going to make it."

Then it occurred to me that the person I was looking at was me. I had no idea I was that bad off. I thought, "Earthquake Kelley, you're gone. When the nurses come in, they're going to find you dead." I didn't feel any sorrow, but I wondered what was going to happen next. Would I just hang around the ceiling? And how could I be at the ceiling looking down at my body that appeared to be dead?

I didn't hover around the ceiling very long. Angels that were so bright they were almost difficult to look at were waiting for me. The angels and the golden vessel carried me gently away as I praised God that I was saved. It seemed that a mere second passed before I found myself in Paradise. The angels took me out of the vessel and I stood next to an angel dressed in gold. That angel said to me, "Walk around."

I cannot find words in my vocabulary to adequately describe what I saw and experienced, but I will try my best to explain it. Indescribable beauty was everywhere I looked. In front of me was lush and perfectly manicured grass that was the most striking green color I have ever laid eyes on. It looked as though somebody had gotten on their hands and knees to cut each blade of grass the same length. Each blade sparkled from what appeared to be a purplish-green jewel embedded in each blade. I walked on the grass and found that it was softer than cotton.

The blades of grass swayed to the music that seemed to be coming from a beautiful building.

The trees were enormous. I saw trees that reminded me of weeping willow trees, and their branches swayed to the music as they appeared to be praising God.

The music and the singing were outstanding. Nothing I have ever heard on earth can compare to the music in Paradise. The sound doesn't simply go into your ears; it permeates your entire body. The music becomes part of your whole being and seems to settle inside of you.

Even the flowers appeared to have a voice. I am an artist, but I could never draw or paint the flowers that I saw. The most beautiful flowers on earth look as though they are drawn with crayons compared to the flowers in Paradise. The colors are more intense and vibrant, and the flowers larger and livelier than anything I have ever seen on earth.

There is not one shadow in Paradise. Radiant light shone with a dazzling brilliance and illuminated everything as far as I could see. With every breath I took, my entire being filled with a fragrant aroma that surpassed anything you can imagine. Everything in Paradise is a breathtaking masterpiece of perfection. There is nothing on earth—and I mean nothing—that can compare.

All my life I had heard about this place, and now I was finally here. God's presence was not only all around me but in me. The beauty is spectacular, and there is an overflow of abundant peace and joy. I felt like I would burst because I was filled with so much joy. I wanted to dance and do handstands. I had never been able to do a handstand on earth, but I knew I could do one now. In fact, it seemed that I had the ability to do anything. I wanted to run and leap into the air shouting, "Thank you, Jesus!" It also occurred to me that I was no longer sick and in pain.

As I continued my tour, I came upon a river that sparkled and shimmered like liquid diamonds. The colors in the water reminded me of expensive stained glass. The soft waves of the river seemed to dance to the music. I couldn't decide if I wanted to jump in the river, drink from it, or just stand on the banks and gaze at the water as I listened to the music.

As I stood on the bank of this crystal river, I thanked God for taking me out of the intensive care unit and away from all the pain. I wanted to stay here forever and enjoy the sights. As I stood on the river bank, I looked across the river and saw another piece of land that was just as lovely as where I was standing. But suddenly I felt a gentle tug on my shoulder as someone pulled me back toward the golden vessel. I sensed that I was not going to stay here much longer. As I was pulled back gently, the thought came to me, "Where is my son Scott?"

The hand stopped pulling to allow me a second look at the other side of the river. It was then that I saw a figure walking toward me. I was thrilled to see that it was my son, Scott! He was as handsome as ever with his big locks of curly hair.

I was elated! I cried out, "Scott, it's you! It's you! You're alive!"

"Yes, Dad, I'm alive."

"Son, this place is really something!"

He replied, "Dad, you and Mom told us for years about this place. It's so much better than anything you described."

I was so excited to see Scott that all I could think was how desperately I wanted to cross the river and hug his neck. "How can I cross over there? Is there a boat or something?" I asked him.

"There's no boat coming for you, Dad. You can't cross this river because you must go back and finish the work God has for you to do. You must go back. Remember when you made me that promise? You're still helping the poor, aren't you? Remember, Dad, you gave me your word."

Seeing my son in Paradise was worth every moment that we spent teaching our children about Jesus and raising them to live for Him. I miss Scott and think about him every day. But it means so much to know that he is in Paradise and not locked up in prison or spending eternity in hell. I know what King David meant when he said, "My son can't come to me, but someday, I'm going to him." If you are a parent, keep preaching the word of God to your children. You will never regret it.

After Scott spoke to me, another man came and stood in front of him. It was Elder Shumate, a man who died in 2002 and was a father in the Lord to me. I said, "Elder Shumate, is that you?"

He replied, "Son, you can't come over to this side yet. Your time is not now. You must go back."

I saw other men and women of God whom I had known on earth. Some were people whose funerals I had attended. Other faces were unknown to me. But all were telling me that I had to go back to earth and finish the work God has for me to do. I didn't want to hear that because I wanted so badly to stay.

A hand pulled me away from the river and I continued walking. I came upon a group of children of all different ages who were running, jumping, and playing. Gary, my ten-year-old nephew, was killed in 2004 after being hit by a car. I looked at these children to see if I could spot Gary. Somehow I knew that he was in that crowd of children.

Then another group of children caught my eye. As I stood and watched these children, I heard a voice say, "You're wondering who those children are." It was clear that this voice was responding to my thoughts.

I was surprised that someone could read my thoughts. I looked around and, although I didn't see anybody, I knew that I was hearing the voice of the Lord. I replied, "Yes, Lord, I am wondering who they are."

"These are children who died from diseases, wars, accidents, murders, and other things that happen to children," He said. "Some were still-births and others died from miscarriages. These are all the children that I brought home to be with me. No harm can ever come to them again."

Then the voice choked back tears as He pointed out another group of children and said, "See those children? I had a plan for their lives. I had things for them to do. But because of the selfishness of sin and the hardness of peoples' hearts, these children were aborted and sent back to me."

He pointed out another group of children and, with the same trembling voice said, "I sent these children to the homes of so-called Christians. I sent these children for ministry. I sent them for exhortation. I sent them to help the world. But their parents listened to the ways of the world. They listened to wrong counsel. They thought they had financial problems and could not afford these children. They had secret abortions, thinking that nobody would find out. But nothing is hidden from me. I see everything."

I could sense the Lord's pain and hurt as He spoke these things. As I listened, I saw a side of Him that I never knew existed. Never before had I realized that He could hurt over His creation. I felt sorry for Him at that moment; it hurt me to feel His anguish.

He continued to speak, "You have a big job to do on earth. You must go back and tell the church of their sins. Tell them that the things they think are hidden are not hidden from me. You must go back and preach to sinners and tell them to repent of their sins."

In my lifetime on earth, I have heard the sounds of sorrow, pain, and despair. I have heard mothers wail in grief upon learning that a child they love has died. But in all my life I have never heard the sound of grief and sorrow like that of the Lord's voice as He spoke about the spiritual condition of those on earth. His voice reflected agony over the sins of His creation.

"Go back and tell people that words have meaning. Tell them that the world has been hiding behind words from the beginning. Instead of saying baby, they call it a fetus. Instead of saying sin, they call it a disease. Warn them that the church and the world have bought into this deception. They have taken the truth of my word and turned it into a lie. Warn my church not to fall for these lies. Warn them of the hardness of their hearts. Tell them that abortions among those in my church must stop. Warn doctors who claim to be Christians but perform abortions that they are terrorists against the unborn."

The Lord reminded me of the time that my father tried to have me aborted. "It was my hand that hid you in your mother's womb." I thanked Him over and over again for protecting me.

He continued His warnings. "There are people who chase sex with such lust that they will pull out by the roots anything that stands in their way. They are running after sexual perversion, going from one relationship to another, conquering every bed they can lie upon with not a care of what I think.

"There are others who have deviated from my word. They no longer seek after me because they want to be accepted by unholy social crowds where there are no morals and no standards. Many have trivialized my word and told themselves that what they are doing is not wrong.

"Tell them that their lives are my business. The kingdom of darkness is after their souls. The enemy starts with their bodies. He wants them to sin to the point that their bodies are withered. He works on their thoughts until their minds are a swamp filled with muck and mire, sending up to my nostrils the smell of rotting flesh. Warn them that this is a trap from the pit of hell to pull them far away from me and my word.

Many in my church have so many secret sins that they are considering suicide. Tell them that if they will repent, I will clean away all of their shame and remove the guilt.

"There are people, even in the church, who don't want to show any untimely blemishes on their bodies. They will do anything to stay young. They idolize themselves, and the spirit behind the worship of self is the kingdom of darkness. Others want money so badly that they are not willing to wait on me. Satan is behind it all."

I pleaded with the Lord to please let me stay in Paradise and to send somebody else with this message. I had all but been shot for preaching deliverance, so I surely didn't want to add a strong warning about sin and the need to live a life of holiness. But the pain in the Lord's voice was more than I could bear. I wept and repented to my Savior for not wanting to return to my sick body in the intensive care unit.

The Lord said to me, "My church is like someone who has a broken leg. Instead of having it fixed, they decide to leave it alone. The more they try to walk, the worse it becomes. It is the same way with my church. There is a spiritual dislocation of my people from me. Sin has caused a fractured relationship and, like any broken bone, it will continue to cause trouble if it is not fixed."

He reminded me of scriptures, such as Romans 6:1-2 which say, "Shall we continue in sin that grace may abound? Certainly not! How shall we who died to sin live any longer in it?"

The Lord continued, "If my people do not repent of this broken bone of sin, it will lead to amputation. This means that people will be cut off from me. You must go back and warn my church of their wicked hidden lifestyle of lust, fornication, and adultery. Tell them to repent.

"Tell them to repent of witchcraft, rebellion, and unforgiveness. Tell them to repent of lying with their mouths and with their lifestyles. They must repent of their hatred toward each other just because of the color of their skin. Tell them to pray; pray from the depths of their hearts. Tell them to fast and to seek my face with all of their hearts."

As He spoke, I cried out to Him, "Father, please forgive me for not praying and fasting the way I once did."

He continued, "There are ministers who are planning to divorce their wives. Some think they need another wife who can help them further their ministry. Some have already decided upon another wife. They are hoping their wives will die so they can marry another person. Tell them it is not my will for them to marry another woman. Until these ministers repent, their ministry will not go forward. Some will die in their sins and their diseases because they have not repented.

"There are ministers who are committing adultery and engaging in homosexuality. Some have a wife, but they have lovers on the side. I have given them many chances to repent and they refuse. They are not serving me. Tell them to repent, or I will remove my breath from their bodies and death will come to them. Some will fall dead behind their pulpits. Many people will see their lifeless bodies hit the floors. Tell them to repent! Repent of their sins and lustful lifestyles! Tell them that many of them are not taking me seriously by living any way they please.

"Warn ministers who are preaching only for money and fame that they will be judged. Tell them that I am removing my hand of mercy from them. Some have set themselves up in ministry that was not of me. Warn them to repent. Tell the hypocrites and the lying preachers and prophets to repent. Warn them all that they will have a place in hell. I have given all of these people a chance to repent. Tell them that if they do not repent, their shame will rock the planet.

"Go back and tell my church that people are holding grudges against me because I have not given them the things they wanted. Some have cursed me in their hearts because I did not answer them as quickly as they wanted. Some have yelled to me while on their knees, 'Why did you let my mother die? You let me down. Why did you let my mother leave me?' Others have cursed my name and vowed never to pray to me again. Some are cursing me in their hearts because their pregnancies ended in miscarriages. Some blame me because they lost their jobs. They are saying to me, 'You don't care! You must want me to be poor!' Some give me a deadline to come through for them or they threaten to do something evil to get money.

"I am being blamed because people are not married. They are saying that it is my fault that they are alone. I am being blamed by some because they were molested as a child. Some believe I allowed men to rape them. They will neither praise nor worship me. They say to me, 'Where were you when I needed you? I hate you.' Until they repent, they cannot be blessed. Nobody can receive from me as long as they are holding things against me. They cannot receive from me and hate me in their hearts. They must repent.

"There are ministers who are holding things against me. Some say, 'Why is it taking so long for my ministry to be launched? Where is my car? Where is my new house? I have cancer; why have you not healed me yet? I am your servant; why is it taking so long?' Until they repent, their ministries will go no further than they are right now. These people treat me as though I am one who sins. Tell them that I am a Holy God who has never sinned. They cannot have anything I have promised them until they repent.

"Many people in the church have held grudges against others for years. Tell them that I will not bless them until they repent and forgive those who wronged them. Many sicknesses in the church are not related to anything in the demonic realm. They are related to bitterness and unforgiveness. Tell them to forgive each other and to repent for holding grudges. Until they forgive others, I cannot forgive them. They will not be healed of their infirmities until they forgive.

"People are seeking my hand and not my face. Go back and tell them to repent. Some no longer see me as their Lord and Savior. They have turned from me. Warn them to repent.

"Many of my people do not believe that I see what they do. And many believe that they can live their sinful lifestyle and enter my holy city. They will not! Tell them that unless they repent, sickness and disease will not leave their bodies. Once cursed by me, no prayer will help them because their sins have placed them under this curse. Unless they repent, they will die with their sicknesses.

"There are people who have listened to my voice and repented on their deathbeds. Many who are thought to have died lost in the eyes of some people are not in hell. They repented before they drew their last breath and are now with me. Some of the people that you saw at the edge of the crystal river heard my voice telling them to repent. They did, and now they are with me in Paradise. Some who thought they were saved when they died are not with me. They are lost in the torments of hell because they did not repent of their hidden sins.

"There are unsaved men who are controlling their families, and they attend church only to convince their families that church is not what it is supposed to be. Their wives are saved, but the men are not. These men criticize the church and dispute my word until the wife leaves the church. The children no longer attend church, either. Many fathers are leading their families to hell. Sinners are dying and going to hell every day. Whole families will be lost and in hell for eternity because they don't know me."

The Lord showed me a vision of people burning in hell's fire. I heard the screams and saw the flames. The fire was so hot that I could feel the heat. I saw the looks of torment on their faces and I knew that many of these were from churches that preached messages only to satisfy the flesh. I saw a whole family—a father, mother, and all the children—in hell. Yellow and red flames covered their whole bodies. They cried out in pain as they bit their arms and pulled on each other, trying to find relief. I felt terrible grief for those families who are lost and in hell for eternity. I knew that I had to do something to keep families from going there forever.

The Lord spoke again. "Son, do you remember when you died of a drug overdose and those evil spirits pulled your soul out of your body and into hell? I spared your soul from hell so I could use you to win others around the world and keep them from going to hell. Can you turn your back on those that will be lost forever unless you minister to them and warn them of what will take place if they don't repent? Many people will be there because they went to church but they never repented of their sins and accepted me in their hearts.

"I am sending you back to tell people to repent of all their sins. Tell them to pray from the depths of their heart. Tell them to fast and seek my face. Unless they repent, they will never see my holy city."

The Lord also showed me cell groups of terrorists—groups of one woman and four men. If I saw them walking down the street, I could point them out to you. He told me that they were already living among the American people, and they were already planning terrorist activities. He also showed me a great flood hitting the city of New Orleans and people dying.

After the Lord finished speaking to me, I turned to my right and found myself standing next to the beautiful golden vessel that had carried me to heaven. A door opened for me and angels smiled at me as I sat down. The door closed gently and, in the blink of an eye, I was back in the hospital bed, once again feeling the pain of the aneurysm.

I started praising God and thinking about the duty and awesome responsibility He had just placed in my lap. As though He were in the room with me, I heard His voice as he whispered, "Take this seriously. You must take this seriously. My people are not taking me seriously. Keep your heart clean no matter what people say or do to you. Forgive them. If you can forgive the man who killed your son, you can forgive those that hurt you in the churches."

Within two days, the doctors sent me home. They could not understand how I survived this brain aneurysm. My Hindu doctor wanted to take me to India and show me off to other doctors.

I came home from the hospital, but my head still seemed to be on fire. We live in the mountains of California, and it gets very cold and snowy there in the winter. I had a fan in the window so I could cool off, and I almost made a snowman out of Selena. My head still had to be packed in blocks of ice. I could not sit up by myself. I couldn't dress myself or walk fifteen feet to the kitchen. I had to eat slowly because my esophagus had shrunk. My food had to be cut into tiny pieces, and often I would choke. Thank God for Selena, who was an angel during my illness. She was always there to help me recover and get my strength back.

Today I am still walking around with a subarachnal aneurysm that the doctors say could kill me at any time. But I will not die until my mission on earth is finished. The enemy wants me dead, but it is God who holds my life in His hands. Only He will decide when it is time for me to go home to be with Him.

The church where I was employed was praying for me, and I was eager to get back to an environment where I could be around other believers. But now I knew that I must obey the Lord and go to Hollywood. Once I had physically recovered, I sat down with the pastor and told him that God was calling me to Hollywood. He hit the roof. He even told me that I didn't hear from God. But I knew what God was telling me: go to Hollywood or die. If I didn't obey, I would continue in rebellion, and I knew that rebellion would be my eternal demise. God had shown me both heaven and hell, and I knew exactly where I wanted to spend eternity. My rebellious days were over.

During that time I received a call from a minister who said, "Earthquake, I have a building in Hollywood. We are moving our church to Beverly Hills, and I'll let you take over the five hundred dollar a month lease on this building."

It is impossible, without the intervention of God, to get any building in Hollywood—especially with a large parking lot—for five hundred dollars a month. God had been trying to tell me for two years that He had a building prepared for me in Hollywood, but I did not have enough faith to listen. Instead of being obedient, I based my decisions on circumstances as I saw them in front of me. I had to take a detour into the wilderness, just like the children of Israel, before I would be obedient and enter the Promised Land.

CHAPTER 8

Living in the Freedom of God's Will

"And the world is passing away, and the lust of it; but he who does the will of God abides forever."

- 1 John 2:17

In May of 2005 we started our church in this building, which is an old theater called The Actor's Playpen. We call the church Bridge of Deliverance. I preach deliverance, and I preach the message God gave me to bring back to the church. We fast, pray, and stay in the Word of God. I don't preach a message of fluff; I preach exactly what the Bible says. I did not particularly want to preach the deliverance message because it brought me great persecution from ministers and people in some churches. But I learned that the people who do not want to hear a deliverance message are often the people who need it most. People everywhere need to be set free from bondage and sin.

Our church is in the heart of Hollywood, which is right next to Beverly Hills. People think the movie stars live in Hollywood, but they do not. The actors and others in the industry simply work in Hollywood. When they drive up to the studios, they must go through a gate with armed security. They work at a city within a city and have no contact with those in the city of Hollywood.

Even though we minister to a few Hollywood actors and stunt men, our ministry is primarily to gang members, runaway children, drug addicts, homosexuals, and others on skid row. We minister to these people, helping them to get delivered and back on their feet. We have a prison ministry and an outreach to the youth. We have seen God heal and deliver so many people.

Our church members stand outside the nightclubs at three o'clock in the morning and, as the young people are leaving, we hand out tracts and tell them about Jesus. We wear shirts that say "The Bridge" as conversation starters. People ask us, "What is The Bridge?" That is my opportunity to give my testimony. I tell them how that I was involved in witchcraft and drugs and how the Lord delivered me.

Racially our church is equally divided, and we have members who came from all walks of life. We have a small church, but many of our members preach. I also encourage the women to preach. My wife preaches, and Selena and I are there to support our members in everything they want to do for the Lord.

I have taught my church elders how to let God use them to set people free. Some people believe God can do what He says He will do, but they don't believe God will use them to do it. I want everybody in my church to be used by God to help people, and I do whatever I can to train them. If God will use me with the background that I have, He will use anybody.

One time I was called to go to a hospital and pray for a little boy who had cancer. I took all of my elders with me so they would learn how to lay hands on people and pray for them without being afraid. This little boy was hooked up to all kinds of machines and he was hemorrhaging from his ears and nose. We knew he was in bad shape, but nothing is too hard for God.

We knelt around his bed and laid hands on the boy. We took authority over the cancer in the name of Jesus. I reminded that spirit that it tried to attack me twice, and I told it to go in the name of Jesus. The grandmother brought us a report that the boy was healed.

I have traveled all over America and to overseas countries preaching deliverance and the message God gave me to preach. But one reason that I believe God placed me in Hollywood is because the area is full of the occult. There are many Gothics who dress completely in black. They wear black clothes, black trench coats, black boots, long black hair, black fingernails, and black paint underneath their eyes. We minister to them. We minister to witches and rockers. We minister to everybody who breathes. And I am glad to finally be in God's will.

Hollywood has been steeped in the occult for many years. I'm sure you have watched television programs with occult activity, but you might not have paid much attention to what you were watching. This has been a problem for years. For instance, consider two of the most successful shows of their day: The Beverly Hillbillies and Bewitched. If you ever watch reruns of the Beverly Hillbillies, notice Granny. She practiced witchcraft on that show. She was a shaman, or a medicine doctor. She practiced water dowsing and she always had a giant barrel with strange ingredients like pickled eye of newt that she stirred counterclockwise with a long spoon. She cast spells on Jethro so he could find a girlfriend, and she put curses on Mr. Drysdale. She made statements like, "I have to get back to the hills to practice my curious arts."

Using a laugh track, the producers always placed laughter over Granny's antics. That is what the enemy does; he makes us think it's all a joke. It's all just innocent and funny, right? It's all a fantasy, right? We laugh while we are being indoctrinated.

The program Bewitched exposed us to witchcraft, astral projection, levitation, and other demonic activities. Baby Tabitha didn't practice the same kind of witchcraft that Endora and Samantha practiced. Tabitha was always in her crib and could never reach her toys. Samantha taught her, "Tabitha, you need to learn how to practice wishcraft." So Tabitha wished her toys to move to her crib.

Many in the church watched and laughed right along with the sound tracks. We need to understand that just because something is funny or shown in a cartoon format does not mean it is harmless. You might think you are playing for fun, but the devil plays for keeps.

Hollywood was founded by people who wanted to have good morals in society. But that didn't last very long. Yes, we had some good programs. But once the people in the film industry started to make money, they ran out of things to do with their money. They were bored people with a lot of money. They could buy everything they wanted, travel the world any time they wanted, and have all the girlfriends and boyfriends they wanted. For something new and exciting, they started hiring people to perform séances and call people back from the dead. Of course, they were not actually calling people back from the dead; they were calling forth demonic spirits.

Then they brought mystics from overseas countries, such as India and Russia. In my opinion, Rasputin, who came from Russia, was one of the most demonic men who ever influenced America. This man's pictures remind me of those of Anton LaVey, founder of the church of satan. Even in their photographs, both men appear evil and demonic.

From dabbling in things like séances and mysticism, the Hollywood elite moved further into the occult. That led them deeper into every other sin imaginable. Some of the Hollywood stars who were deeply involved in the occult died at a young age. Jayne Mansfield, for example, was involved with Anton LaVey and the church of satan. Jayne was scalped at the age of thirty-four in a tragic automobile accident. LaVey claimed that he placed a curse on her boyfriend, who was killed in the same car accident.

These people wanted something that made them feel good, offered a hint of spirituality, and gave them power. They wanted to control and manipulate. Their whole outlook on life was, "I'm going to do what I want to do and you can't stop me." That is still the prevailing attitude today.

Cecil B. DeMille was against this kind of movement, so he began to produce films with a Christian theme. Two of his films were Exodus and The Ten Commandments. Not everything in his movies was biblically accurate, but at least he made an effort.

Unfortunately, DeMille could not get enough Christians to support his films. Today, much of the programming that comes out of Hollywood is smut. How many good, wholesome shows are on television right now? How many clean and family-friendly movies are produced? The industry has hardly been able to produce a movie or a television program without pushing sex and indecency, violence, the occult, the homosexual agenda, or foul language. I thank God for the handful of decent, family-friendly movies and programs, but I wish there were many more.

With all the filth, temptation, and demonic activity in and around Hollywood, it is not easy for people to remain faithful to God. For many folks, it is a constant struggle. My desire is to start a school of deliverance so that I can teach people everything I know about deliverance. Jesus came to set the captives free, and people from all corners of the earth—not just Hollywood—need to learn how to get their families and other people set free from the bondages of sin.

Evil spirits don't go away just because we refuse to acknowledge them. In the sixth chapter of Ephesians, the Apostle Paul warned the body of Christ about the danger of our unseen enemies, and he told us to fight by using the armor of God. Satan sets many traps to destroy us, but we don't have to fall in them. Here is an analogy I like to use. Suppose you are driving down a dark road at night. The bridge ahead is washed away but there is no sign to warn you. As you approach the bridge in the dark, the bridge is not there and you cannot stop your car quickly enough to keep yourself from going over the edge and into the water. That is how a trap of Satan works.

But thankfully, we don't have to live without a sign. God has given us plenty of signs to warn of impending danger; they are found in His Word of Truth, the Holy Bible. They are revealed to us through the power of the Holy Spirit. God always warns His children, and He gives us every tool we need to overcome the enemy.

We must stay in proper spiritual shape by reading and rightly dividing the Word of God. We must remain holy and pure before the Lord by repenting of any sin in our lives. We must do those things to keep the enemy under our feet. We can recognize the enemy and cast him out in Jesus' name. But we can't do it if we don't live righteously and know our enemy.

The church must also be willing to accept those who need deliverance. We live in the mountains of California where there are bears, snakes, coyotes, and other wild animals. Recently a wildcat got into our garage. I could have called animal control, but I decided to take care of the situation myself. I took a fishing net and a big stick and went into the garage where I planned to corner the wildcat and kill it.

I had the wildcat cornered when I saw sandaled feet and a robe appear between me and the cat. Then I heard a voice say, "Why are you trying to kill this cat? This cat came to your garage for protection. It feels safe in your garage. I sent this cat here to teach you a lesson. I want you to preach this message everywhere you go. Tell my church that I send hurting people to them. They come to you for protection. They come because they need a place where they can feel safe. But too many of my people are trying to kill those that I send to them. Tell my people to care for the hurting people that I send to them and not to harm them."

I repented for trying to kill that wildcat.

Where are people, including Christians, supposed to go when they have problems and need deliverance? Do they go to the church? Do they even want to confess to the church that they are having these problems? In most cases, the answer is no. Instead, they continue to battle hidden sin. Or they visit psychologists. Maybe they will even call the psychic hotline.

That is why God is raising up those who know how to help people who need to be delivered. It is the saints of God who need to help these folks. All around us are people who have been in torment and bondage for too long. Instead of criticizing them, gossiping about them, ignoring them, or running them off, we need to help them receive deliverance.

Some people say we shouldn't preach a deliverance message because we're talking about things that make people feel bad. "Preach a positive message," they say. Please hear me. Every moment of every day, people are dying lost and going to hell. What is more positive than wanting to keep people out of hell? I've been to hell. And I don't want anybody else to go there.

I have been tormented, and I have heard the cries of those who are tormented and lost forever. If you spend eternity in hell, you constantly will be reminded of what a fool you were for listening to the devil's lies. You will replay every sermon you ever heard. You will remember every person who gave you an invitation to turn your life to Jesus. And you will spend eternity begging for another chance.

Over and over, you will ask yourself, *"Was selling my soul to the devil worth it? Was sleeping with all those women worth it? Was stealing that money worth it? Was preaching heresy worth it? Was living in rebellion and unforgiveness worth it? Now I'm doomed to hell. Was it worth it?"*

God does not want any person to perish. He wants all to come to repentance. Sometimes there is a little bit of good in people that will pull them toward God like a magnet. When people are bound by evil spirits, they are in torment. And torment hurts. The enemy is never satisfied with a little bit of torment. His goal is to kill, steal, and destroy. Sometimes in their hurt, tormented people will reach out to God.

Even as you have been reading this book, people have died lost and are in hell for eternity. For them, the harvest is past, the summer is ended, and they were not saved.

If you could have reached even one of them with a message of the power of God to bring salvation and deliverance, would it have been worth it?

CHAPTER 9

Who's Watching the Children?

"Therefore you shall lay up these words of mine in your heart and in your soul...you shall teach them to your children, speaking of them when you sit in your house, when you walk by the way, when you lie down, and when you rise up."

- Deuteronomy 11:18-19

One thing that motivates me to teach people about the enemy's schemes and devices is the fact that he tormented me for years and stole my childhood. I look back now and think, "It's payback time." I don't want any child to go through the torment that I went through, so I want to teach parents about the enemy's schemes so they can protect their children. As much as the following chapters of this book are for parents and adults, they are equally important for young people who are old enough to make decisions to either live righteously for Jesus or live rebelliously for Satan.

First Peter 5:8 says, "Be sober, be vigilant; because your adversary the devil walks about like a roaring lion, seeking whom he may devour." Just as a lion attacks the lonely, the weakest, and the youngest, the devil tries to devour those who are young, alone, or spiritually weak. That includes your children. And he will stop at nothing to consume them.

I see so many parents—even Christian parents—who allow their children to be exposed to things and situations that can cause them serious problems. Often this is simply a lack of knowledge on the part of the parents. But don't forget the Bible's warning that God's people are destroyed for lack of knowledge. Perhaps I risk sounding alarmist, but I hope I can give you information in this chapter that will help you protect your children from the enemy that seeks to devour them.

If you pay attention to the news at all, you know that child sexual abuse is a serious problem. Recent statistics from the FBI's National Incident-Based Reporting System indicate that sixty-seven percent of sexual assault victims are under age eighteen. Thirty percent are age eleven and younger. Some victims are assaulted by relatives, babysitters, and other people whom the children trusted. They are assaulted by people who are skilled at preying on children.

The demonic spirits that attack these children as a result of sexual abuse will cause them to become tormented adults who suffer from a host of problems—depression, anxiety, drug and alcohol abuse, eating disorders, promiscuity, and the list goes on and on. Only the power of the Holy Spirit through salvation and deliverance can bring freedom and relief from the oppressive guilt, shame, and torment.

It is a tragedy that, right here in America, there are churches where pedophiles seek out boys and girls. On the surface the people might seem very kind, while all the time they lurk about, looking for an opportunity to strike. One of my wife's relatives encountered a man in church who attempted unsuccessfully to seduce him. That man, who preyed on children, eventually died of AIDS.

So many children in the churches today do not have fathers who are active in their lives. Predators come after them because they know that these children are starving for affection. After the predator has offered affection and gained their trust, the sexual abuse begins.

Predators know that churches are always looking for volunteers, so they view church as the perfect site to target children without arousing suspicion. The problem is so widespread that some churches now run police background checks on potential employees and volunteers. Many churches have implemented standards to reduce the risk of child abuse. These are all excellent ideas. There are also Internet-accessible databases that give the names and locations of registered sex offenders in your area.

Children everywhere are at risk, and parents must be cautious about the people they allow around their children. A parent must be able to spiritually discern the character of those who are caring for their children. Never leave them alone with somebody you do not know or trust.

Another problem I want to address is the things you bring into your home. If you want to protect your children, do not allow anything into your home that is evil, violent, or occultist. That includes toys, books, movies, and computer or video games. If you allow such items into your home, you might one day regret the things your children do after being exposed to them and having their minds saturated with this garbage.

Every year we collect donations of toys for inner city children. A manufacturing company donated a box of toys that originally were intended to be given away as part of the kid's meal at a chain restaurant. These were monster space toys and I had a bad feeling about them. Instead of giving them away, I decided to throw them away. I took them home and sat the box at the side of my bed until I could throw them away on trash pick-up day.

That same night, I heard something tapping on the side of my bed. Selena and I listened closely and wondered what the loud tapping noise was. I turned on the light and didn't see anything. Then the Holy Spirit said to me, "It's the toys in the box." I threw those toys away immediately and the tapping stopped.

Evil spirits attach themselves to these kinds of demonic toys. I recommend that you not bring anything like that into your home; and if you have something like this in your house, throw it away. Don't sell it and don't give it away. Burn it, throw it away, hammer it to pieces, or do whatever is necessary to keep it out of somebody else's hands.

It never hurts to pray before you buy a toy. If the toy is affiliated with a movie that deals with witchcraft or anything that is evil or demonic, my advice is that you keep it out of your house. If the toy looks demonic, it probably is.

Neither should children be allowed to watch movies that contain the occult, sex, or violence. (Adults shouldn't watch them, either. The same demonic spirits that attack children also attack adults.) Supervise your children's television watching, and take the television out of their bedrooms. When I was young, I was watching television late one night and saw a demonic spirit jump out of the television and jump back in. Here I was, looking for a place to escape from these spirits, and I couldn't even watch television and find relief.

Today you can turn on your computer or walk into a store and choose from a selection of hundreds of video games that simulate death and violence. There is one game that teaches you exactly how to rob a bank, and it includes instructions on the type of guns to use and whom to shoot first. There is another game called "kill Bush." Why would you allow your children to play a game that teaches them how to rob a bank or kill the President of the United States?

People who develop these games are involved in witchcraft and all types of perversion. They are evil and demonic, and these games reflect the evil that lies within them. The people who produce these games are against everything that Christ stands for; as Christians, we should not be supporting their evil efforts. Furthermore, when you bring those things into your home, you are allowing those same evil spirits to enter your domain.

When you play games that simulate death and violence, a demonic spirit attacks you. Matthew 24:12 tells us that in the last days, the love of many will wax cold. This demonic spirit causes you to have a cold, careless attitude toward humanity. It gradually destroys your compassion for people until you care nothing about others.

Eventually that person will be attacked by nikttiel, the spirit that causes rage. When this spirit attacks a person with rage, an otherwise normal teen-aged boy will bring a gun to school and shoot students and teachers. You will hear the media say, "This boy was troubled. Did he receive proper medication and psychiatric care? Did he have a brain tumor?" In response I say, "The boy was demon possessed." You might hear people say, "He was such a nice boy. I never would have expected him to do anything like that." Sure, he might have been a nice boy. But when rage grasped and controlled him, it was a monster too big for him to handle. It's too big for *anybody* to handle without the blood of Jesus and the power of the Holy Spirit.

In the beginning, one small spirit will attack that boy. As he continues to engage in sin, more spirits will attack. Eventually he becomes possessed, and the spirits order him around and control his every move. He hears voices muttering, "Try this. Do this." The goal of these spirits is to open a trap door and lead this boy straight to hell.

Christian children are not immune from attacks of the enemy; even they will get burned if they play with fire. Shock rocker Marilyn Manson, who took his name from a combination of Marilyn Monroe and Charles Manson, once attended a Christian school. But he dabbled in things he should have never touched until eventually he became ordained as a reverend in the church of satan. His music was said to have influenced the Columbine High School killers. Manson wears ghoulish make-up and performs macabre stage acts. His music talks about death, suicide, hurt, hell, fear, selling your soul, haunting, violence, and drug use.

The mother of actor River Phoenix was once an independent Christian missionary. But River Phoenix became so involved in drugs that he speedballed every drug he could take. At the age of twenty-three, he collapsed and died of heart failure on the sidewalk outside of a nightclub. An article about him in *Life Magazine* included a picture of him in the casket. He was wearing a black T-shirt and was contorted into a sideways position. The article said that his parents had given up on him. What a tragedy when parents give up on their children.

Here is something that is controversial, even in Christian circles, but I believe you should also be careful with books such as the *Harry Potter* series. Since people find the books entertaining, they tend to view them as harmless fantasy. But the author is on record stating that she consulted with witches when writing the books, so please understand that what you read is very real. If children begin to experiment with using a magic wand and casting spells, they are dabbling in the occult and opening a door that could lead them deeper into the occult and demonic influence or possession.

The Harry Potter series revolves around magic, wizards, and witchcraft. There is an underlying message that people who don't believe in magic have a medieval mentality and are intolerant, mean, ugly, and stupid. We are told of a classroom book entitled *The Standard Book of Spells*. There is mention of levitating off the ground. We learn that aminagi are those who can transform themselves at will into animals. Harry owns a cloak that makes him disappear. We are left with the impression that wizards, witches, witchcraft, divination, levitation, curses, and casting spells are all perfectly acceptable as long as they are done for good and not evil.

Some of the classes offered at Hogwarts School of Witchcraft and Wizardry are divination, unfogging the future, and casting spells. Two magazines mentioned in one book are Transfiguration Today and The Daily Prophet. Do you remember from Matthew 17 that Jesus was transfigured on a mountain? And how many times is the word prophet mentioned in the Bible? Do you see how someone who lacks spiritual knowledge might be confused about the source of witchcraft power?

When some children read these books, the idea of learning divination, casting spells, speaking curses, disappearing behind a cloak, and using a magic wand holds great appeal. Someone even wrote on a website, "I would like to learn to be an aminagi because it could prove itself a useful skill." When someone wants to learn to change from human to animal form, you can be sure that an evil spirit will show up, eager to teach his student that "useful skill."

Interestingly, the third book of the series, *Harry Potter and the Prisoner of Azkaban,* accurately describes the tormenting effect that demonic spirits have on people, although the author never calls them demonic spirits. She calls them dementors—apparently a combination of the words demon and tormentor. They are described as the foulest creatures on earth; they infest dark places, glory in despair, and drain hope, peace, and happiness. Although they don't see them, even people who don't believe in witchcraft can feel their presence. We are told that a dementor will feed on you until you are reduced to something soul-less and evil.

The book describes the prison as a place where people are trapped inside their own heads, incapable of a single cheerful thought. It tells us that most go mad within weeks, and they sit in the dark muttering to themselves. But we are told that, when they let you out of the prison, it's like being born again. It's the best feeling in the world. We also learn that dementors aren't keen on letting people out of their prison.

That is a surprisingly accurate description of the effects of tormenting demonic spirits. People who are bound in the occult experience the effects of these evil spirits, so how many of the witches with whom the author consulted are themselves dealing with these foul spirits? How many have been reduced to something soul-less and evil? And how many leave that prison and become born again?

When the Harry Potter books became popular, so did books on casting spells. With the release of each new Harry Potter book, spell books were often prominently displayed in the children's section of bookstores. These books are written and illustrated to attract young people. Here are the promised benefits from one of these books: The spells in this book can help you increase your popularity, protect you against bullies and harmful gossip, win at sports, stretch your time, and bring answers to mind during a test.

What young person wouldn't be intrigued? Doesn't everybody want to be popular? Doesn't everybody want to be protected from bullies and harmful gossip? To win at sports, have more time, and know the answers to all the test questions?

This book also promises to help you achieve goals and to use amulets to draw friends to you, while protecting you from those who would not be friendly. It teaches incantations and gives you a secret magical name. The "fun, beautiful guide" is a great introduction to the "power of positive magic."

Need I tell you that this originated in the pits of hell? Right here in America, you can walk into the children's section of a bookstore and purchase a book that encourages and trains your children in "positive" witchcraft and sorcery! Instead of teaching their children to pray, serve God, and depend on His help through every situation, people teach their children to take matters into their own hands and receive assistance from demonic spirits.

Sometimes it is necessary to prayerfully research these things so that you can study to show yourself approved and learn about the enemy's plan of attack. But if you are not doing it for that reason, leave it alone. Don't be like the man that I once heard say, "I must investigate the power of the devil. One must know the strength of the devil before he can be conquered. If one is to move toward the light, one must experience its opposite, which is evil."

How ridiculous! That's like taking poison just so you can have a near-death experience and appreciate having your stomach pumped. Here's my advice: stay away from the poison. It's real, it's dangerous, and it will harm you. Demonic spirits will attack and begin to control your life, and you will find yourself doing things you never thought you would do. It's the law of diminishing returns. First you play violent video and computer games. Spirits attack, and eventually you become a violent person who is full of rage. Your next step is to take your rage out on other people. And finally, you kill someone.

Or maybe you dabble in Wicca and cast a few spells. Then you start doing séances and calling forth spirits that you think are people coming out of the grave. You levitate and draw pentagrams on the floor. You try illegal drugs because all your friends are doing it. The enemy will always make the next step look very enticing. Unless you repent and turn to God, you will move deeper and deeper into sin, bondage, and torment.

Parents, watch children who tell lies. One of the things God hates is a liar, so lying should be taken seriously. Children who fall into the traps of Satan often begin by lying and practicing deceit. From lying, the child will find other things to get away with. Evil spirits are activated when you lie; they begin to manipulate people and circumstances.

"Who took my cell phone?" you might ask.

"Not me," the child replies.

If the parent doesn't deal with that kind of lie, it will eventually become, "Why were you late for work today?" And instead of admitting you stayed up late and hit the snooze button on your alarm clock too many times, the answer might be something like, "I had a flat tire on the way to work and it caused me to drive over an embankment."

You keep building up your box of lies. The evil spirits get in the box with you. And once the enemy steps in, he takes over. Lying is one of the keys to the realm of darkness. It is my opinion that every person who is involved in any form of the occult started out as a liar. Once you become comfortable in the fairy tale world you have created through lying, then demonic spirits take you from one fantasy world to another where you will have power beyond your imagination. That demonic spirit will make an offer and say, "What do you want? Name it."

And the child might say, "I want to be a magician. I want to be better than Houdini. I want to walk through glass and make elephants disappear."

The spirit says, "I can help you do that, but first you must agree to do everything I tell you to do."

Here is where you have the choice to run from the enemy or make a deal and sell your soul. Remember that Satan tried to tempt Jesus by offering him all the kingdoms of the world and their glory, if only Jesus would fall down and worship him. Jesus quoted scripture and told Satan to get lost. We need to do the same.

How do you handle children who lie? Proverbs 13:24 says, "He who spares the rod hates his son, but he who loves him disciplines him promptly." When a child lies, you should discipline promptly and without anger or frustration. There is no justification for beating a child, but spanking a child's bottom is not going to harm the child. It gets the foolishness out of him. Proverbs 22:15 says, "Foolishness is bound up in the heart of a child; the rod of correction will drive it far from him."

Children should not be punished for making a mistake, nor should they be punished because a parent wants to vent anger. But children should be spanked for foolishness. Some children will learn to behave with alternative forms of discipline. But with most children, spanking is a fast and effective way to halt misbehavior.

I saw a picture of a woman sitting on a sidewalk next to her son who was wearing a sign that said, "Hi. I'm thirteen years old and I steal. I want to go to prison to be with my daddy."

That mother was obviously at her wits end. But she should have been spanking the foolishness out of her son when he was a child. Now that he is a young teenager, the foolishness is still in him and she is trying to shame him into straightening up. Proverbs 19:18 tells us, "Chasten your son while there is hope, and do not set your heart on his destruction." It is a sign of love when you use biblical methods to straighten up your children. What decent parent wants their children to end up in prison or dead because of foolishness?

Raising children is an enormous responsibility, and every parent needs God's guidance to perform that important task. Be loving and communicative, and discipline with patience and love. Pray over your children daily. Ask God to place a hedge around them and protect them from accidents, molestation, abuse, disease, injury, and harm. Speak words of encouragement over them by repeating the promises of God's Word. Bless and never curse them.

Instead of reading wizardry or fairy tales to your children before they go to sleep at night, read the Bible or a good Christian story. Don't let them go to bed having filled their minds with the story of a girl who was almost eaten by a wolf. In the occult world, the nighttime hours are called bewitching hours, and that is when evil spirits come into the house to torment children. Before they go to bed, fill their minds with things of God and pray with them.

If you want the peace of God in your home, the most important thing a family can do is stay in church, pray regularly, and nurture their children in the admonition of the Lord. Dedicate your children to God at a young age. Teach them to obey you, because that will train them to be obedient to the Lord. Your own life and conduct should set a godly and upright example for them to follow.

Early in life, bring them into a personal relationship with Christ. Teach your children that God loves them and has a plan for their lives. The words of God in Jeremiah 29:11-13 are wonderful words to speak over your children. The New Century Version reads, "I know what I am planning for you, says the Lord. I have good plans for you, not plans to hurt you. I will give you hope and a good future. Then you will call my name. You will come to me and pray to me, and I will listen to you. You will search for me. And when you search for me with all your heart, you will find me."

If you have done all that you know to do and your children falter along the way, never stop praying for their deliverance and salvation. Stand on the words of Proverbs 22:6, "Train up a child in the way he should go, and when he is old he will not depart from it." Speak over their life and say, "The devil will not have my child. My child will become a man or woman of God. As for me and my house, we will serve the Lord."

Always show them love and always intercede for their salvation. My own life is proof that you cannot underestimate the power of a parent's prayers and spoken blessings in the life of a child.

CHAPTER 10

There's Something in My Room

"He who sins is of the devil, for the devil has sinned from the beginning. For this purpose the Son of God was manifested, that He might destroy the works of the devil."

- 1 John 3:8

Have you ever looked at your child and wondered how he became so ill-natured and where he learned to do such outrageous things, especially when you are certain he didn't learn it from anybody at home? Psalm 51:5 tells us that we were conceived in sin and shaped in iniquity. What causes all of us, even from a young age, to have a propensity to sin?

The Haitian witch who taught me voodoo had a better understanding than most Christians of how we are shaped in iniquity. She taught me that low level demonic spirits dwell in every hospital and wait for children to be born. The spirit actually grabs the head of the baby, right alongside the person who is delivering the baby. A demonic spirit is assigned to each child, and the job of this spirit is to teach the child to do evil. First and foremost, it teaches the child to lie, then to cheat and steal. Psalm 58:3 says, "The wicked are estranged from the womb; they go astray as soon as they are born, speaking lies." These demonic spirits even have a favorite classroom, and where do you think it is? Right there in your child's room, especially at night.

Not long ago I heard a minister on national Christian television say, "There is nothing in your child's room at night. Your child is not seeing anything." That minister is wrong! God bless you if you have never seen anything in your room at night; but there are many people, including children, who have.

All across the world, children are tormented at night by evil spirits. I was one of them. And I pray for children who are tormented at night by these spirits. Even though you might not be teaching your child voo-doo—and I hope and pray you are not—that does not mean your child is exempt from torment by evil spirits. In this chapter, I will explain what your child is experiencing and tell you, as the parent, how to deal with it.

The primary spirit that attacks children at night is the waster spirit. In the islands of the Caribbean, the waster spirit is called the bogey man. They teach that the bogey man is a hideous and monstrous man who torments children at night when they don't behave. In America, people call him the boogie man. How many times have you heard somebody say, "If you don't be good the boogie man is going to get you?" *Never* say that to your children. By saying that, you are cursing your child and giving the waster spirit permission to attack your child. Be careful what you speak!

The job of the waster spirit is to cause you to waste away, little by lit-tle. This is the spirit that caused me to get only two hours of sleep a night for many years of my early life. I had nightmares constantly, and I would awaken only to see the same spirit from my nightmare standing in my closet laughing at me. The waster will stand in the doorway and haunt the child all night long. It will even block the doorway to the bathroom so that your child fears going to the bathroom and wets the bed. During the day, it reminds the child that he is going to be tormented when he goes to bed that night.

On October 17, 2006, the *Chattanooga Times Free Press* printed an article entitled "Scary Dreams" and subtitled "Dream analyst says chil-

dren's nightmares are natural." Following are the highlights from that
article:

Nightmares become more common this time of year (Halloween) as fami-
lies decorate the yard with tombstones, tune in to horror flicks, and shop
for costumes featuring bulging eyeballs. And while children's nightmares are
generally nothing to worry about, you don't want your child haunted by dark
images night after night, according to dream analyst Lauri Loewenberg.

"Children start experiencing nightmares between ages three and five,"
Loewenberg said. "If your child starts getting nightmares, they are right on
track. The reason they start getting nightmares is because he or she is realizing
that bad things can happen—the nightmares are the way they start to process
negative things in life."

The analyst gave parents these recommendations. First, if your child
is jolted awake from a nightmare and shows up at the foot of your bed,
the first thing you need to do is reassure the child that it's not real. One
suggestion to help your child overcome, according to this dream analyst,
is to imagine turning those big mean eyes into balloons. Another suggestion is to have your child use his Harry Potter wand to turn the monster
into a teddy bear.

If your child has nightmares night after night, this dream analyst sug-
gests that it may be an indication of an underlying issue. For example,
there may be a bully at school. Or perhaps their goldfish died.

What did you notice about that article? First, even a secular dream
analyst admits that occult objects and horror flicks cause nightmares.
But she neglected to mention that these nightmares can be demonic attacks caused by allowing those evil spirits access to your home.

The second thing you'll notice is that the analyst knows that it is
common for children as young as three years of age to have nightmares.

What she failed to mention is that three to five is the age when demonic spirits can begin to effectively take control of your child's life.

But look at the solutions the analyst offered. First, you are to tell your child that the nightmares not real. And what about the recommendation that your child use a Harry Potter wand to perform magic? Or the suggestion that the underlying cause of nightmares stems from something that happened in the child's life, such as a goldfish dying?

If a parent relies on any of these secular recommendations, the child is still going to be tormented. The demonic spirits behind nightmares are very real. And please understand that you cannot use magic to make evil spirits leave. Demonic spirits will not leave until a believer in Christ takes authority over them in the name of Jesus and commands them to leave.

If the waster spirit is not dealt with, it will eventually move from night torments to house haunting. You might hear noises at night, perhaps footsteps in the attic or objects crashing in the house. Again, if not dealt with, the child will grow up to become a fearful and paranoid adult who might suffer from panic attacks. A fearful and paranoid adult experiences constant stress and often feels that life is on the brink of a catastrophe. Fearful people who live with constant stress, panic, and paranoia risk dying prematurely from stress-related diseases, such as heart attacks.

Another spirit that children deal with is the big face spirit, which has a very large face and no visible body. It often attacks children who have a call and an anointing of God upon their lives. Its purpose is to offer the child the opportunity to live a life of sin—through the occult or through drugs, for example. This spirit will offer the child anything related to a life of sin, just so the child will not fulfill his destiny in Christ.

Pay attention to children who have strong disciplinary problems. This spirit will teach children how to gain power over their parents and other adults. If your child embraces this spirit and begins to do what the spirit instructs, you will find yourself dealing with a very unruly child who could eventually become an evil child. This is a child who has the potential to kill others. This spirit will say, "Enough is enough. Get a gun and kill them." It will give the child step-by-step instructions on how to destroy people.

The third spirit that children deal with at night is the pillardoc spirit, which is the spirit that came into my room, carried me through a window pane, and offered me the opportunity to become a wealthy bank robber. This spirit will say to a child, "If you follow me, I will support you in this effort. I will help you rob banks and make sure you don't get caught." I even watched this spirit split itself into several different spirits, each of which will attack other family members.

When there is trouble brewing between the parent and child, these spirits move right in. If the child is being abused at home or ridiculed at school, these spirits view this as an open door of opportunity. Evil spirits enjoy this kind of conflict because it gives them a greater chance to succeed in their efforts. The big face spirit will have them involved in gangs, alcohol, and drugs. The pillardoc spirit will promise the child fame, power, or whatever it thinks the child might want.

If your child obeys these spirits, they will own your child. They will control the child until they finally knock the pillars out from under him. When that happens, something tragic will occur. Perhaps your child will get caught at his evildoing and spend time in jail. He might become a drug addict or even a murderer. Or he might commit suicide.

There are other spirits that can attack children, but those who are being tormented at night are primarily dealing with these three spirits. As a parent, what should you do?

First of all, if your child has nighmares, or is afraid to stay in his own room at night, or tells you there is something in his room, always investigate. That builds up confidence in the child that the parents believe and care about him. In the spirit realm, nighttime is a different world. You would not send your children to an African jungle by themselves at night, but many parents send their children to the demonic spirit realm alone at night.

What does a parent often do in response to a child's nighttime fears? They turn off the light, shut the door, tell the child there's nothing in the room, and order the child to stay in bed. It the child gets up and comes into the parents' room at night, they send the child back to bed. The child has no choice except to lie there in the dark and be tormented. He will sleep with the light on and his head tucked under the covers.

Don't allow that to happen! You are your child's protector and it is your responsibility to take care of your children, even at night. If you suspect that your child is being tormented but is not talking about it, ask. If your child is wetting the bed or telling you that he is afraid to go to the bathroom at night, ask these questions: Is there something in your room that is making you uncomfortable? Is anything bothering you at night? Is something making you afraid to go to the bathroom? If there is, tell me so that we can pray over your room.

Spirits can be in your child's room, but the child will not necessarily see the visible manifestation of a demonic spirit. They might simply feel an eerie presence in the room. Even black spots and hoops that appear in the room and on the ceiling at night are an indication that the waster spirit is in the room.

All a parent has to do is investigate, and these spirits will realize, "Uh oh. Somebody's checking up on me." Go to your child's room and say, "I might not see you, but my child says you are here, so I know you are here. I know who you are and I know why you're here. The blood of Jesus defeated you and every evil spirit at the cross. I am going to anoint my child with oil and pray, and I am covering my child, this room, and our home with the protection of the blood of Jesus. You cannot torment my child any longer. I command you, in the name of Jesus, to leave this place and never return."

Sleep in the room with your child once or twice, just to give him assurance. Every night before your children go to bed, pray with them. And I don't mean a now-I-lay-me-down-to-sleep prayer. Pray a serious prayer over them. Anoint their heads with oil. Read something from the Bible. Take authority over those spirits and let them know that they are not welcome in your home.

Be sure to destroy everything in your house that is remotely demonic. Teach your children that these things open the door to the demonic realm, and that you, as a family, cannot keep anything in your home that allows these evil spirits an open door. Don't let any space get between you and these evil spirits. Any parent who takes this kind of action will see a dramatic change in their child's behavior. And once the light of God shines on the dark demonic realm, there is no place for evil spirits to hide.

Psalm 91:5 says, "You shall not be afraid of the terror by night." Teach your children that, as long as they have Jesus living in their heart, they are not to fear evil spirits because greater is He who is in you than he who is in the world. The Holy Spirit, who lives in every believer, is stronger than any demonic power from hell. Tell your children to say the name of Jesus and the evil spirits will have to flee. Lead your children to Christ at a young age and instill in them the knowledge that they have authority over these evil spirits.

John 8:32 tells us, "You shall know the truth and the truth shall make you free." The word "know," in that context, means to perceive, to realize, and to gain knowledge. To "make you free" means to liberate and deliver. Once you gain knowledge and realize what is going on in a situation, then you can use your authority to be liberated and receive complete deliverance.

Parents, it is your responsibility to get control of this situation. Do not allow your children to be tutored by demonic spirits; get the teacher out of the house. You might be sound asleep while your child is being trained and tormented by evil spirits. If your child becomes diabolic and gets involved in all kinds of activities he shouldn't be involved in, it's a sure sign he is being influenced or trained by evil spirits. These spirits won't leave until they are forced to leave. And if they never leave, they will destroy your child. It doesn't matter that you are involved in church or ministry. In fact, to the enemy, it's better if you are active in church or ministry because a rebellious child reflects badly on you.

My own daughter Cherish and my son Chris were terrorized at night, and Selena and I took authority over the spirits and fought for our children. After that, both slept soundly through the night with the lights off.

Children are being destroyed by the enemy every day. All children need somebody to stand in the gap and intercede for them, just like my mother did for me. Anoint their heads with oil. Speak the blessings of God over your children. Never say things like, "You're going to be a no-good bum, just like your daddy." Demonic spirits are listening to the words you speak over your child, and they are ready at a moment's notice to attack your child.

Parents, you might decide that you'd rather believe the minister on television who tells you that there is nothing in your child's room at night. But believing that evil spirits do not exist or ignoring the problem is not the answer. Closing the blinds so you don't see them only makes the room darker. And evil spirits thrive in both physical and spiritual darkness.

If you are an unsaved parent, or if you are a Christian who is living with unrepentant sin, you have no authority over any of these demonic spirits that are invading your home. That authority is available only to a believer in Christ who is living a holy life. But somebody who is a believer—perhaps a grandparent or another relative—needs to stand in the gap and take immediate action for the child who is being tormented. In fact, you should pray over the children from the moment they are conceived to limit the influence of these evil spirits in the children's lives.

To the churches in America and around the world, I believe it is important that the church pray over their expectant mothers and the children they are carrying. Speak the positive words of God over the lives of these children, even before they are born. Parents, never speak ill over an unborn child. By doing so, you are cursing the child before he or she is born and giving demonic spirits permission to influence and torment your child. The enemy is ready to attack these children from the moment they exit their mothers' wombs, so why not take an offensive posture by praying and speaking blessings over the children before they are born?

When you take action according to the word of God, you can stand on the words of Isaiah 54:17: "No weapon formed against you shall prosper, and every tongue which rises against you in judgment you shall condemn. This is the heritage of the servants of the Lord, and their righteousness is from me, says the Lord."

Stay on guard, live a holy life, pray over your children, and speak the Word of God into their lives. Force these evil spirits to flee before they have a chance to ruin your child's life. And just as importantly, live your own life as a man or woman of God so that you can positively influence your children and close the doors of your home to the enemy. All children deserve to grow up in a godly home where they can be loved, nurtured, and taught to live mightily for the Lord.

CHAPTER 11

Illusionists: How Do They Do That?

"The coming of the lawless one is according to the working of Satan, with all power, signs, and lying wonders, and with all unrighteous deception among those who perish, because they did not receive the love of the truth, that they might be saved."
- 2 Thessalonians 2:9-10

Sometimes Christians—even those who think they are always on guard—can be tricked and deceived by the enemy. One of the enemy's devices is to leave your mind in wonder and amazement at his schemes. You might not even realize it is one of his schemes. When that happens, you have opened a door just enough for him to slip inside. Second Thessalonians 2:9-10 tells us that the work of Satan will be displayed in all kinds of counterfeit miracles, signs, and lying wonders, and in every sort of evil that deceives those who are perishing.

Throughout history and still today, we see the enemy practicing his deception through a form of magic known as illusion. The dictionary defines illusion as "an unreal, deceptive, or misleading appearance or image; or a false perception or interpretation of what one sees." It can also have the same meaning as hallucination.

Illusionists are people who walk on water, make buildings disappear, swallow razor blades and pull them out through their abdomen, or cut people in half with a buzz saw. When you watch an illusionist perform, you are not hallucinating. Nor are illusionists entertaining under a false perception; they are operating under the direction of demonic spirits.

These demonic spirits imitate the actions of God's angels and His Holy Spirit. For example, just as God has sent His angels to hide smuggled Bibles from the eyes of border guards, the enemy has hidden things as large as the Statue of Liberty by using a cloaking spirit. Just as God can protect from physical harm His children who have sold out to Him, so Satan can protect from physical harm demon-possessed people who have sold their soul to him.

What is demonic possession? In First Chronicles 12:18, the Spirit of the Lord came upon Amasai, an officer in David's army. In Judges 6:34, the Spirit of the Lord came upon Gideon. In both of these references, the original Hebrew text tells us that the Holy Spirit clothed Himself with these men. In other words, the Holy Spirit took possession of Amasai and Gideon and wrapped Himself with them. When the Holy Spirit takes possession of us as children of God, we are able to operate in a supernatural realm that surpasses anything we otherwise would be capable of doing.

This is important to understand because demonic spirits imitate the Holy Spirit and act in a similar fashion. They, too, can clothe themselves with people and take possession of them. When demonic spirits take possession of human beings, those people can also operate in a supernatural, albeit demonic, realm.

People who are involved in the type of magic known as illusion likely dabbled in the occult early in life. Perhaps they had parents who were involved in witchcraft, new age, or other forms of the occult, and it seemed perfectly normal for them to walk in the house and see their mother levitating off the floor with her eyes rolled back in her head. Or they might have dabbled in the occult because they didn't have a father at home, and they were searching for something that offered validation and power. Other people believe that by exploring the occult they are exploring the darker side of life. And only by exploring the darker side will they find spiritual enlightenment and understand the meaning of darkness. In the beginning, their occult activity might have seemed harmless.

That is how the enemy traps you into the occult. On November 1, 2006, *Publisher's Weekly* reviewed a book on Haitian voodoo. Here is part of that review: "Vodou (voodoo) is not what most people think. It's not devil worship, dark curses, and drumbeat-driven orgies performed at midnight, poking needles at dolls, or simple superstition. Of course, it is not without its dangers, since the Iwa (deities) can wreak a frightening vengeance. It's not foolproof, either; without proper initiation into addressing the Iwa, they will simply ignore you. This book will give potential initiates the proper tools for communicating with the deities of vodou..."

Sounds harmless as long as you handle it properly, doesn't it? I suppose the nuclear bomb is harmless, too, as long as nobody touches it. But once somebody drops it on you, life as you know it is over.

Voodoo, witchcraft, and other occult activities might be harmless, too, as long as nobody touches them. After all, the enemy can't accomplish his evil deeds unless he works through people. When people become involved in the occult, in the spiritual realm they are dropping nuclear bombs. Once you touch these things, they will wreck your day, your life, and your eternal future.

The enemy is looking for a small crack in the door so he can push his way into your life. Have you noticed how that, when you open your door in the summertime, every fly in the neighborhood finds its way into your home? You don't have to open the door far or keep it open long. And once the flies are in the house, they pester you until you get rid of them. That is exactly the way the enemy operates. Crack open the door to sin and evil spirits will rush in to influence and torment you.

The popular illusionists that you have seen over the years have opened the door of their life to the enemy and become so deeply involved in the occult that their bodies have become demonic spirits wrapped in human flesh. Unless they repent, turn their life to Christ, and allow the Holy Spirit to replace the demonic spirits that are holding them captive, they are unlikely to live a long life. The enemy typically operates on a ten- or twenty-year contract. And once a person begins their journey with the devil, their days on earth are numbered.

Harry Blackstone, Sr. vowed at the age of twelve that he would some-day become a great magician. In his time, he was billed as the greatest magician the world had ever known. Blackstone was the first person to cut someone in half using a buzz saw. He performed "illusions" such as lifting the decapitated head of his female assistant from a cylinder, stealing wallets from audience members, floating a light bulb, and causing a handkerchief to dance and a birdcage to disappear. He toured the United States and set box office records in cities across America. After Blackstone died, his son carried on the show until his own death in 1997.

The world's most well-known magician may have been Houdini. He performed many slight-of-hand tricks that involved cards, ropes, or disappearing coins. Houdini had early involvement with mediums and worked for a brief period as a psychic and a clairvoyant. One of his famous acts was the Hindu needle trick in which he swallowed dozens of needles and thread, then regurgitated the needles with the thread inserted into the eyes of the needles. He made a ten thousand pound elephant disappear on a lighted theater stage. And he became known as an escape artist who, after being handcuffed or chained, could free himself from anywhere, whether it was a prison cell or a padlocked crate that was thrown into a river. He also walked through a brick wall.

Houdini's homes in New York and Los Angeles were said to be haunted. Even after his Los Angeles home burned to the ground, the site was haunted by ghostly apparitions.

Houdini spent the later years of his life exposing fraudulent psychics and séances, which caused trouble for him in those circles. During a 1924 séance, a medium channeled a spirit that spoke this threat over Houdini: "I put a curse on you now that will follow you every day for the rest of your short life." Houdini died on Halloween, October 31, 1926 at the age of fifty-two.

Houdini's wife performed séances in her unsuccessful attempts to bring him back from the dead. The Houdini Museum still performs séances to often sold-out audiences. They state that their museum has been haunted for years.

One well-known illusionist was admitted to the Society of American Magicians at the age of twelve. This man defines magic as the art of controlling events by supernatural power. He—through a cloaking spirit—has caused the Statue of Liberty to vanish. He has walked through the Great Wall of China, levitated across the Grand Canyon, and caused audience members to disappear and then reappear in unexpected locations. His performances have set box office records.

There are two young men that I will not name who are on the scene today performing illusionist magic. One of these young men is considered by many to be an illusionist much like Houdini. He performs in Las Vegas, New York, California, and on more than one television network.

He has walked on water; flown off the roofs of buildings; walked vertically up the side of a building; crawled through glass windows; dived through another person's body; hung in the air by fishhooks that were threaded into his body; and impaled or pierced himself in ways that would normally cause severe bodily injury or death. Yet through all of this, he walks away unscathed.

From an early age this young man was interested in mysticism, which is a doctrine of the occult. He believes that, through mind control, he can perform acts that defy nature. In other words, he believes that he can use his mind to perform miracles and other astonishing feats.

His performances are described as groundbreaking. Those who see his live performances are shocked speechless and wide-eyed with disbelief. Some fans call him their idol and want to take him home. And almost everybody asks incredulously, "How does he *do* that?"

The secret behind feats like this is demonic spirits. This young man, through the influence of early occult activity and evil spirits, sold his soul to the enemy at a young age. I know because I've been there. I know because a Haitian witch, a voodoo priest that I called Dad, and a demonic spirit guide taught me how these things work. As a young boy, I did not ask the pillardoc spirit to carry me through a glass window and offer me the opportunity to become a wealthy bank robber. I did not learn astral projection by sitting on the front pew of a church every Sunday. All of that happened because of my involvement in the occult.

It is these same demonic spirits—evil spirits that clothe themselves with people—that keep illusionists upright as they walk on water or levitate off a roof. It is demonic spirits that allow illusionists to walk through a brick wall or crawl through a glass window pane. And it is demonic spirits that allow these people to saw themselves or others in half without killing themselves.

Just as the Holy Spirit of God dwells in and with a believer who serves Christ, so do demonic spirits dwell in and with those who serve Satan. When these spirits clothe themselves with a person and live inside their body, they are settling into the space that God intended to be occupied by His Holy Spirit. And just as the Holy Spirit of God protects a believer in Christ, so do these demonic spirits protect one of their own.

Think of the drunk driver who veers his car into another vehicle, killing one or more passengers. Yet the drunk driver walks away without a scratch. Firewalkers walk across hot coals of fire without burning their feet. Tibetan monks sleep outdoors in snowy mountains with no blanket and temperatures below freezing, yet they do not freeze to death. They are able to withstand almost any pain that the enemy causes them to inflict upon themselves.

But make no mistake. These people are being tormented day and night by demonic spirits. The enemy of your soul is an evil taskmaster. Once you have entered his realm, he will make you follow every order. He will use and abuse you. He will make you believe there is no turning back. He will do his best to convince you that you can never be free. He will kill you before your time. Then his evil spirits will drag you into hell where you will be tormented for eternity.

Just because someone seems to be enjoying their involvement in witchcraft—or any other sinful activity—does not mean they are not being tormented. Satan is a wonderful campaigner with an experienced and well-trained staff. But once you've voted for him, the truth comes out. You learn that he is a liar, a deceiver, and a destroyer. You learn that it is impossible to satisfy evil spirits that possess you; they always demand that you do more. You start by sacrificing a cat; but before your life ends they make you sacrifice a person. Then they make you sacrifice your own life. Every new act moves you to a deeper level in the demonic realm.

So it is with illusionists. The enemy is having a heyday with these folks. He even enables one young man to walk on water and imitate a miracle of Jesus! And since this illusionist also wears a cross around his neck, people are confused about the source of his power. On one website, someone inquired about his religious beliefs and commented: "I'm confused. He prays and wears a cross, but his logo resembles a pentagram. He does things that resemble Jesus Christ, like walking on water. I am in awe over him. He truly mesmerizes me and I am a Christian."

Christians mesmerized by demonic spirits? What is wrong with this picture? We must be alert to the enemy's devices because, as I mentioned at the beginning of this chapter, one of his tricks is to leave your mind in wonder and amazement at his schemes. He wants you to open a door just enough for him to slip inside.

In countries throughout the world where people practice witchcraft, voodoo, or idolatry, strange demonic manifestations occur frequently. It is not unusual for people to levitate, change into animals, or fly through the air—with or without a broom. People in these countries know without a doubt that spirits are involved. Those who understand and fear the spirit world keep their distance from those who engage in occult activities. When a woman changes into a bird and collides with a car before changing back into a woman, everybody knows she is a witch. They are so fearful of the spirits that they will not even come close enough to assist her as she lies injured in the street.

But here in America, we pay hard-earned money to watch these same destructive and evil demonic spirits perform through people. We give them multi-million dollar performance contracts. We hire them to entertain us at birthday parties and trade shows. Many times they perform to sold-out audiences. I can almost hear the laughter and mockery that bursts forth from these demonic spirits every time another person buys a ticket to watch them perform.

When people sell their souls to the devil—when they agree to obey demonic spirits in return for whatever enticement they have promised—the enemy will gladly train these people to enter his wicked realm. Sure, you can curse people and cast spells. Sure, demonic spirits can lift and carry you as you levitate off the floor and walk on water. You can even turn yourself into an animal or make an animal disappear. Is that power? Yes, but it's power straight from the kingdom of hell. Before these illusionists die, they might perform some acts that will make your hair stand on end. But is it worth dying before your time and spending eternity in hell?

Where does it all end? When you work for Satan, he ravages your soul. At the end of the job, he takes your life. If you never give your life to Christ and receive His deliverance, you likely will die early from a mysterious illness, an accident, a drug overdose, or your own suicide. I knew a man in Beverly Hills who was living a very ungodly lifestyle. He dropped dead suddenly and unexpectedly from a rare disease that is found only in the jungles of the Amazon. How do you think that disease reached Beverly Hills from the jungles of the Amazon?

Ecclesiastes 7:17 tells us, "Do not be overly wicked, nor be foolish; why should you die before your time?" Be assured that if you are overly wicked and foolish, you will die before your time. Your only hope is to have someone—perhaps your mother or another godly relative or friend—interceding for you in prayer until the Holy Spirit opens your eyes and you receive salvation and deliverance.

If you are reading this and you are involved in any kind of occult activity, please understand that everything the enemy is telling you is a lie. Jesus Christ can and will set you free if you will only ask. When you accept Christ and receive deliverance from your involvement in witchcraft, black magic, white magic, new age, satanism, voodoo, or any other form of the occult, of course the enemy will try to lure you back. You once belonged to him, and he will be enraged that he lost you to Jesus. He will lie to you and try to ambush, manipulate, and seduce you so that you will give up on Jesus. If he doesn't succeed with that, he will use people—even other Christians—to force you to compromise your message.

Satan hates the fact that you are familiar with his weapons of mass destruction. He doesn't want you to testify of your deliverance or see others receive deliverance. Satan might be a great campaigner, but he's a sore loser. Don't worry, though; Jesus already fought that battle for you and won. The devil can't have you back unless you give yourself back to him. Praise God for His mercy and grace, His protection, and the weapons He gave us to keep the victory!

A devout believer in Jesus Christ—even those who have never been involved in occult activity—will always be a target of Satan's wrath. But God has given us every tool that we need to keep the enemy under our feet. A demon might show up, but an angel of God shows up, too. I have commanded demonic spirits to leave in the name of Jesus, and then watched as they screamed and ran away in terror. Through the name and the blood of Jesus, every child of God can live in victory.

When you live a holy life; when you pray and fast; and when you read and obey the Word of God, you have no reason to fear the enemy's tactics. He cannot gain an advantage over you when you know his strategy and resist him. Remember the words of James 4:7, "Submit to God. Resist the devil and he will flee from you."

The Bible also tells us in 1 John 4:4 that "He who is in you is greater than he who is in the world." No evil spirits are more powerful than the righteous, Holy Spirit-filled believer who knows how to use his spiritual authority through Jesus Christ. We should be thankful that He has not left us defenseless!

CHAPTER 12

Gateway to Hell

"Marriage should be honored by all, and the marriage bed kept pure, for God will judge the adulterer and the sexually immoral."
- Hebrews 13:4 (NIV)

Earlier in the book I mentioned that I was only five years old when the Haitian witch taught me about the spirits that attach themselves to people who have sexual relations outside of marriage. From a young age I knew that this opens a gateway to hell. The marriage bed is covered by God; the unmarried bed is not. When a man and woman come together in the bonds of marriage, the Bible says that they become one flesh. God protects the marriage bed because it is part of God's covenant, and the enemy hates God's covenant.

What is a covenant? It is a permanent bond or relationship that is based on trust. When God makes a covenant with His people, He makes a pledge with them that lasts forever. Through covenant, God establishes and confirms His relationship with us.

But there can be no covenant until there is first a sacrifice. Before Jesus offered His own life as the sacrifice, people offered animals. The animals were cut in half and arranged opposite each other, with enough room to pass between the two pieces. As they passed through the sacrifice, the people pledged to remain irrevocably bound to the covenant. They established the pledge by saying, "If I am unfaithful to my covenant, may it be to me like these animals." They understood that if they remained faithful to the covenant, they would be blessed. If they did not, they would bring a curse upon themselves.

Before we come into covenant with God, we must first pass through the sacrifice, who is Jesus. In Galatians 2:20 the Apostle Paul wrote, "I have been crucified with Christ and I no longer live, but Christ lives in me." In other words, our old self dies and we become one with Christ.

A covenant is different from a contract. The parties to a contract agree that, as long as all act according to the provisions of the contract, it will remain in force. A contract becomes void if it is violated or terminated. When God established marriage, He did not base it on a contract. A man and woman who marry become parties to a covenant. They make a vow of commitment before God. They pledge to die to self, to become as one flesh, and to remain together until they are parted by death, no matter what circumstances come their way.

Even witches understand that God will never break His covenant. If the covenant is broken, God's people must break it. Satan and his demonic forces despise God's covenant—including His marriage covenant—and they will do anything possible to destroy it.

One way the marriage covenant is destroyed is through sexual activity outside of marriage. If people knew what they are subjecting themselves to, they would not engage in this activity. When people engage in sin outside the marriage covenant, they have no protection against any of these demonic spirits. Their life becomes an open gateway to hell.

There is a principality spirit (erzulie) that has authority to dispatch other demonic spirits once unmarried sex has opened a gate to hell. When I visited Haiti in 1993, I saw this spirit materialize in the visible realm. This spirit is active in places around the world where voodoo is practiced. When thousands of people in a small nation beat drums, dance, call forth demonic spirits, enter a trance, and then have sexual relations with each other, you can imagine how bound by demonic spirits these people are.

You don't want any of these spirits to gain a foothold in your church. If they do, they will start with the weakest person in your church and move through the congregation. The church leadership must be willing to deal with this kind of situation immediately; if they don't, terrible things can happen. I knew a pastor's son who always targeted the weakest girls in the church and had sexual relations with them. This man had a call of God on his life to preach; but money and sex were all he ever talked about. He attended church only to find spiritually and emotionally immature girls to sleep with. This man was in his mid-fifties when he dropped dead in his shower. He lived alone, and somebody found him days later with the shower still running.

Thousands of spirits are assigned to this sin, but I will explain what happens when a person becomes possessed by any of the major spirits.

The bisexual spirit (dantolien) is directly connected to the occult. Most people who are bisexual either are or have been involved in witchcraft or other occult activity. People do not have to experiment sexually with both males and females to become bisexual. Nor do they first have to dabble in the occult. If they have sexual relations with somebody who is involved in the occult, this spirit can attach itself to them through transference of spirits.

Gomorra, a spirit that affects the brain, often comes through sexual activity outside of marriage. This spirit causes adults to act childish, immature, and empty-headed. They forget what they have done just moments after they have done it. They are either late for appointments, or they never show up because they forget dates and appointments altogether. This has nothing to do with conditions such as Alzheimer's disease, dementia from old age, or brain tumors. Gomorra affects people who have no medical reason for losing their memory.

This spirit causes people to perceive themselves as ugly. To feel better about themselves, they have sexual relations with anybody who shows them attention. When that feeling of validation wears off, they seek somebody else to give them attention. Gomorra causes people to become vain and have multiple plastic surgeries. Perhaps they have been married several times, and often they dress like a teenager. This spirit affects both men and women, but a man often tries to validate himself by impregnating several girls, which gives him the approval of other men in the neighborhood.

One of the reasons God destroyed the perverted cities of Sodom and Gomorrah was for their selfishness. Gomorra causes people to selfishly think of nobody but themselves, and it causes them to seek the approval of man. Our approval comes from God, and our minds should be stayed on Him and transformed by His word. Until a person deals with gomorra on the brain, that individual will never benefit from a church service or learn anything from the word of God.

Upper and lower battalions are spirits that attack your body and bring disease. Lower battalions are spirits that attack your blood with all sorts of blood-related diseases, such as AIDS. Imagine them as little soldiers that march right into the blood. The Bible tells us that the life of all flesh is in the blood. When these spirits attack the blood, they bring death to the flesh instead of life.

When I was growing up, I knew a family that was very sexually active with people to whom they were not married. Every one of these people eventually died of a blood disease. Even then I knew what caused their death because I had been trained to know the connection between illicit sexual activity and blood diseases.

Upper battalions attack organs—the heart, liver, kidneys, and so forth. I am not suggesting that every person who develops a disease of the organs did so because they led a sexually active life outside of marriage. What I am saying is that people who have engaged in sinful sexual activity throughout their lives will often find themselves dealing with blood diseases and diseases of their organs.

Fornix is a spirit that causes people to become cold-hearted. When two people first engage in illicit sexual relations, they think they are so much in love. But if cold-heartedness works its way into their soul, that same love they thought they had for each other turns into detachment or even cruelty. People who develop cold-heartedness typically place the blame for the pregnancy on the other person. A man might accuse the woman of being unfaithful and demand a blood test to prove the child is his. Often he will disappear from the life of the woman and child. His heart has closed and it happened when he opened a portal to hell.

Sometimes you see this spirit in people who were once married to each other. Let's say that children were born in the marriage, but one spouse begins a sexual relationship with someone outside of marriage. The husband and wife divorce, and the person who was guilty of adultery wants little or nothing to do with their children from the former marriage. These people can remarry and treat the new spouse's children just fine. But they neglect or even reject their own flesh and blood.

God is able and willing to deliver people from all of these spirits; but often, cold-heartedness is allowed to settle and grow. And it can grow to the point that one person commits murder against the other. Have you ever seen a situation where one spouse kills the other and people are shocked because they never dreamed it could happen? Often that is caused by fornix—a spirit of cold-heartedness.

Skyx is the spirit that causes jealousy and hatred. Most people who are involved in witchcraft believe that hatred comes from spirits that reside around the skyx river, or the river of hate. Witches teach that this river is the lake of fire in hell itself.

Jealousy can eat away at someone's soul until the hatred becomes so intense that one person harms or kills another. Or perhaps the man contracts a transmittable disease and becomes so filled with anger and hatred that it becomes his goal to spread the disease to as many other people as possible. Jealousy, hatred, and cold-heartedness are so common that we can barely pick up a newspaper or watch a news report without hearing of its evil effects.

The hydra head spirit one of the most difficult to deal with. This spirit has the body and tail of a lizard, but it has from seven to nine separate snake heads. Each head has its own unique personality and voice. People who are possessed by this spirit will often both talk to and answer themselves, as though they are carrying on a conversation with someone.

This is the spirit that causes multiple personalities, and it is possible for a person to have more than one of these spirits. Each separate spirit brings seven to nine more personalities. When a person is being treated for multiple personality disorder, the psychiatrist will often say, "Who am I talking to today? Am I talking to George? Am I talking to Sam?" The truth is that the doctor is not talking to a person; the doctor is talking to demonic spirits that have their own voice and personality but are speaking through that person.

People who are bound by these spirits can have counseling every day for the rest of their lives and take every prescription drug on the market. None of those things will work. These people are dealing with a strong spirit that comes out only through prayer and fasting, salvation, and the power of the Holy Spirit. There is nothing else that will deliver a person from these demons.

Demonic spirits have something that I call sensors. A person can walk through the mall and the spirit within them will identify another person who is possessed by a hydra head spirit. The two of them gravitate toward each other. When they engage in illicit sexual relations, the number of spirits in both of them multiplies. These people have the potential to become possessed with hundreds of hydra head spirits and have just as many different personalities operating through them.

Perhaps that sounds impossible; but the Bible speaks of a man in the tombs who was possessed by at least two thousand demonic spirits. When a person is possessed with many spirits that have their own personalities, each spirit has its own voice that talks to the person. When all of these spirits talk and give orders at the same time, the possessed person often will do terrible things. He might become a serial killer who writes rambling notes that make little sense, or he might commit suicide just to get relief from the voices.

Predators cannot imagine what they are doing to innocent children when they attack them sexually. Let's say that a pedophile uncle who is possessed with this spirit has relations with his niece. Those spirits will attack that child; and unless she accepts Christ and receives deliverance, she will likely suffer with multiple personalities when she grows up.

Here is a case of someone who was bound by this spirit through sexual abuse as a child. Barry (not his real name) and his siblings were so abused as children that they were removed from their home and placed in foster care. Barry's foster father sexually abused him, and Barry ran away from their home as a young teenager. He was befriended by an older man who also sexually abused him. For much of Barry's teenage life he lived on the streets. To survive, he did the only thing he knew to do. He sold his body as a male prostitute to older men.

Thirty years into adulthood, Barry was still being treated for multiple personality disorder. He was seldom able to hold a regular job because of his diagnosed "mental disability." As for Barry's siblings, one was sentenced to prison and two committed suicide. Barry's secular psychiatrist often told Barry that he, too, would likely commit suicide.

Satan and his demonic forces hate Barry. They hate the fact that he was created by God in His image. Demonic spirits began their attack on Barry when he was born and they never stopped. They will do anything to latch on to every person who is just like Barry and keep them from accepting Christ as their personal Savior and receiving deliverance.

When someone has been involved in illicit sexual activity for years—even when the activity was forced upon them, such as in Barry's situation—these hydra head spirits will keep a viselike grip on this person when they try to come to Christ. In Mark 9:26 we read where Jesus cast a demon out of a boy, and the King James Version of the text says that the spirit rent him sore. In that context, rent means "to tear or convulse." After the spirit screamed and left, the boy appeared to be dead. That is what these evil spirits do. The tail of this spirit wraps itself around the person's belly area and holds on so tightly that the person thinks something is tearing their insides apart.

When I have prayed for people who are possessed by this spirit, I have seen this horrible demonic creature materialize in the visible realm. Each time I pray for these people, they scream and grab their abdominal area. The Bible says that from the belly shall flow rivers of living water. That is why demonic spirits attach themselves to a person's belly. They wrap into their innermost being and hold tightly because the demonic spirits want to occupy the place that the Holy Spirit should hold.

These spirits know that once the person accepts Christ, the kingdom of darkness has lost that soul to the Kingdom of God. These spirits will be forced to give up the position they hold in that individual's life when the Holy Spirit kicks them out and takes over. Salvation and the power of the Holy Spirit will loose these demons and force them to flee.

Incubus and succubus are two demonic spirits that rape people. Even in medieval times, people knew that incubus attacks women and succubus attacks men. Strangely enough, it is not necessary for these spirits to possess a human body for a rape to occur. The spirits themselves are capable of raping a person without using a human's body to do so.

One night I saw the succubus spirit enter our bedroom. It was clothed in a red dress and wore long red fingernails. At first I had no idea what I was seeing and, for a quick moment, I thought perhaps it was our daughter. But when the spirit turned to look at me, I immediately knew it was not my daughter. The Holy Spirit quickly revealed that I was seeing the demonic succubus spirit, so I commanded it to leave in the name of Jesus and it vanished.

I don't often preach about these two spirits; but the few times that I have, someone has come to me after the service and told me of their attacks by one of these demonic spirits. I always tell them to take authority over it and command it to leave in Jesus' name.

One day I received a call from a minister who fought my deliverance message and was, in part, responsible for my decision to leave the ministry and move my family to New York. He told me that he was attached by one of these spirits, and he apologized for everything he had ever said about me. This married pastor later committed adultery with a single woman and she became pregnant. It destroyed his church.

One of the enemy's powerful methods of killing, stealing, and destroying is by using sex outside of marriage. It wrecks the lives of unmarried people, including teenagers. It destroys marriages and gives the enemy a foothold in the lives of divorced parents and children.

Sometimes the door to sex outside of marriage is opened when men become involved with pornography. A man might think he is innocently looking at pornography and can stop anytime. But the enemy plays for keeps, and soon he finds himself bound in that sin. He can't stop with pornography, so he begins to have sexual relations with someone to whom he is not married. Without repentance, salvation and the power of the Holy Spirit, the man can become bound with evil spirits.

Consider the plight of the young girls who were raped by the gangs in my Stamford neighborhood. If a girl who experiences that kind of torment does not allow Jesus to come into her life and heal her emotions and bring deliverance, she will eventually become controlled by evil spirits. She might develop hatred toward men, become a prostitute, turn to illegal drugs, or spend her life in prison. Her life will be ruined because a gang of selfish, evil punks were looking for gratification.

Then there is the issue of homosexuality. Today society tells us that homosexuality is normal and that people are born that way. That is a lie of the enemy; homosexuality is caused by attacks of demonic spirits. In our state of California, homosexuals have the shortest lifespan of any group of people. Often they die or commit suicide by the time they are forty years old. We are led to believe that homosexuals commit suicide because the rest of society does not accept their lifestyle. That, too, is a lie of the enemy. Let me explain why they commit suicide.

At some point in that person's life, a demonic spirit took up residence. It was a spirit that causes people to experience intense loneliness and to believe that life is not worth living. As they experience further hurt, the door opens to another spirit called atarroth adder, or crown of snakes. These demonic snakes wrap themselves around a person's head like a crown and slowly squeeze. The spirit squeezes until the person is con-vinced he can no longer deal with the pressure. Then he kills himself.

The crown of snakes does not attack only homosexuals, nor does it attack only people who are engaged in immoral sexual activity. Anybody who is under so much stress that they feel unable to cope with life is likely dealing with an attack by this demonic spirit. This spirit can also cause migraine headaches.

I believe that thoughts of homosexuality often begin with demonic spirits that attack someone's mind after sexual molestation or experi-mentation. The enemy will lie to someone and cause that person to have an overwhelming thought that he is homosexual. Demonic spirits will say, "You were born that way. There's nothing you can do about it. Ac-cept it. Ignore those who tell you that homosexuality wrong."

An overwhelming thought that one is homosexual could come from something as simple as a father mocking his son and calling him a derog-atory term for a homosexual, simply because the son prefers playing the piano over hunting. Demons are listening; and once the seed is planted, the enemy delights in tormenting the son and planting thoughts in his mind that he must be homosexual. Once an individual has been molest-ed, experimented with homosexuality, or even entertained the thought that they are homosexual, there are spirits that will gladly attempt to engage the person in that lifestyle.

I grew up with a boy who was not homosexual in the beginning. But his family left him in the hands of an older man who sexually abused him, and that experience changed him completely. Eventually he became a male prostitute who stood on the streets waiting to be picked up by someone in a passing car.

Demonic spirits within homosexuals recognize these same spirits in other people. You might have heard someone say, "That guy is gay; he just doesn't know it yet." The person who made that remark might have seen the visible manifestation of a demonic spirit trying to move onto an individual. If that word is spoken over a person, somebody needs to command that spirit to leave in the name of Jesus, and then plead the blood of Jesus over that person's life.

Many homosexuals have nobody praying for them, so they succumb to these spirits. Here is where the church has made a mistake. Instead of praying for homosexuals and taking authority over demonic strongholds, we have allowed ourselves to become intimidated by people who want to convince the rest of society that this lifestyle is normal. By either teaching that homosexuality is not a sin, or conversely, scorning homosexuals to shame, the church is allowing them to die lost every day. That makes the devil ecstatic. He wants us to pat homosexuals on the back and tell them everything's going to be okay, while all the time he is dragging them straight to hell by the noose he has placed around their neck.

Instead of criticizing and becoming self-righteous, we should look at these people with the compassion of Jesus and say, "What happened to get you in this condition? Jesus loves you and wants to deliver you from all of that. Nothing is too hard for Him. I'm going to pray for you."

If you have a child who is homosexual, go to Matthew 17:21 and Mark 9:29 which say, "This kind comes out only by prayer and fasting." Fast and pray from the depths of your heart for your child's deliverance. Speak to that mountain. Say, "You mountain of homosexuality, you will not have my child. You will come down, in the name of Jesus. The blood of Jesus has made us free, and I declare freedom for my child through the precious blood of Jesus. My child will accept Christ and serve the Lord."

Keep speaking those things that are not as though they are. If God has given you a promise over your child but the child is not living in that promise, speak God's promise over them anyway. Never let the enemy discourage you and cause you to give up, and never abandon your child. Love them even when they are unlovable. Keep telling them that you love them, Jesus loves them, and you are praying and fasting for their deliverance. They won't want to hear it, but tell them anyway.

Sin lies at the door and desires each of us, but God told us to rule over sin. When you repent of your sins and accept Jesus as your Savior, He will close those gateways to hell that you have opened. Jesus bore all of your sins on the cross, and He is waiting for you to repent of your sins so that He can reverse the curse that sin has brought into your life. God wants you to receive deliverance from sin and bondage, and He will help you if you will come to Him in repentance and ask.

Once you have repented, continue to grow in the Lord and don't allow the enemy to regain that foothold in your life. When you accept Christ, you receive deliverance from evil spirits. The Bible says in Luke 11:24-26, "When an unclean spirit goes out of a man, he goes through dry places, seeking rest; and finding none, he says, 'I will return to my house from which I came.' And when he comes, he finds it swept and put in order. Then he goes and takes with him seven other spirits more wicked than himself, and they enter and dwell there; and the last state of the man is worse than the first."

When you accept Christ, the enemy will tempt you and try with all his might to win you back. If you submit to God and resist the devil, he must flee. But what shape will you find yourself in if you turn your back on God and give access to demonic spirits more evil than the ones you had before you accepted Christ?

CHAPTER 13

Keeping the Enemy Under Your Feet

"Therefore submit to God. Resist the devil and he will flee from you. Draw near to God and He will draw near to you. Cleanse your hands, you sinners; and purify your hearts, you double-minded."   *- James 4:7-8*

There has been a debate within the church over whether or not a Christian can be possessed by demonic spirits. What we should be talking about instead is what happens to Christians who allow unrepentant sin to enter and control their lives. You might be the Bishop of a five thousand member church; but if you are flagging down prostitutes in the red light district, there is a good chance you are demon possessed.

Not everybody who says, "I'm a Christian" is truly a born again believer in Christ. Anybody can call themselves a Christian, but not all of those have a relationship with Christ. The enemy wants to control people under the guise of Christianity so that others will have a false impression of our Christian faith. He also wants to convince those who call themselves Christians that they're all bound for heaven when they die, regardless of how they live on earth. Demonic spirits can possess and control those who are far from Christ yet call themselves Christians.

It's unfortunate that, even within the church, we find people who are possessed by demonic spirits. One time after speaking in a church, I was at the altar praying for a woman when an elder's wife came forward and, in a deep and demonic voice, said to me, "You can't have her."

I found myself having to cast evil spirits out of the elder's wife.

Along with possession, let's talk about association. With whom are you associating? Are you associating with God? If you haven't prayed a real prayer in months, then with whom are you associating? When the church has a prayer meeting but you choose to play golf instead, with whom are you associating? When you go all week without praying, reading your Bible, attending church, or spending time in the presence of God, what are you? If you are living with unrepentant sin, what are you?

Here is what you are: someone who is setting yourself up to be toppled by Satan. When you can't find time for God, you have already become lukewarm. When you live with unrepentant sin, you have already backslidden away from God and turned toward the enemy. The Bible says that if we confess our sins, God is faithful and just to forgive us of our sins and cleanse us from all unrighteousness. But the problem is that many people are not clean from their unrighteousness.

We read in Psalm 51:2 that, after the prophet Nathan confronted David about his hidden sin David prayed, "Wash me thoroughly from my iniquity and cleanse me from my sin." How often do we pray that prayer? We should tell the Lord that we want to be holy before Him. We should not desire to live in sin or have any of these evil spirits tormenting us.

Demonic spirits can possess, influence, oppress, depress, and do just about anything else that you allow. If you turn away from God and continue to live with unrepentant sin, you can have all of the above. You can have your choice of thousands of demons, plus a host of diseases. And as long as you continue to live in that condition, you have no authority over these demonic spirits. As I know from personal experience, they will laugh in your face.

Demonic possession is the presence of an evil spirit that has wrapped itself with you, as mentioned previously. This spirit is controlling your life and will continue to do so until you repent. Think of oppression as an evil spirit that is speaking lies or influencing you, or hanging onto your back while harassing or depressing you.

How might a Christian become oppressed by demonic spirits? It can happen when we fail to use our authority and our weapons—such as the Word of God—to fight the enemy; when we fail to take an offensive position and keep the door closed to the enemy; or when we turn away from God and live with unrepentant sin. How might a person become possessed by demonic spirits? It can happen when we allow unrepentant sin to rule our lives.

Sometimes we struggle for years with a particular sin, and often that struggle is caused by a generational curse or by a sin that was committed against us in our past. I'll use myself as an example. As a child I lived with rage over the actions of my father. For the first ten years of my Christian life, I carried that rage. A wonderful minister finally confronted and counseled me, telling me that I could not continue to live my life wanting to beat up everybody who crossed me the wrong way. I had to get deliverance from the temper and rage that controlled me.

Rage is caused by a demonic spirit called nikttiel. One of the lowest manifestations of rage is an attempt to intimidate others, while one of the highest manifestations is a loss of self-control that often leads to violence. Sometimes the person will have no memory of the violent act they committed. Rage causes a person to overreact, scream and yell, or hit people, animals, and walls. Rage will cause a person to insult, injure, and humiliate others. Instead of apologizing for their behavior, they attempt to justify it, while having no sense of remorse for their actions. Besides being a sin, rage will cause serious health problems. You might say that a person who is full of rage is slowly committing suicide.

Like many other sins, people often don't want to admit that they have a problem with rage. But here are some signs: if people leave the room when you enter, or if the mere sound of your voice causes others to cringe, then you have a problem with rage. If you hold grudges for weeks, months, or even years, then you have a problem with rage. If you are a bully, if you criticize people for every little mistake, if you always seem to be angry about some offense against you, or if you become upset over trivial things, then you have a problem with rage.

I have even heard ministers stand behind the pulpit and preach with a spirit of rage. It is evident when they preach that they are angry about something.

Because of past hurts, many Christians have problems with their emotions, and those problems can cause us to sin. But we cannot live our lives blaming others or blaming our past for all of our problems. God does not want us to be emotionally immature and out of control. He does not want us to premeditate evil actions toward somebody; nor does He want us to allow a person to have so much power over our lives that we think or say things that cause us to sin. We cannot give everybody a piece of our mind. As the saying goes, if you keep giving people a piece of your mind, you won't have much left.

Before I left Stamford as a teenager, I hit a guy in the head with a light bulb. Today he is a grown man and, even though I have apologized to him and asked his forgiveness, he still wants to kill me for embarrassing him thirty-five years ago. What a shame to live with offense and allow another person to have that much control over your life.

We need to study scripture and ask God to show us how to properly manage our emotions. When we have a problem, we should recognize it, admit it, and take it seriously. We should repent and ask God to forgive us. Regardless of how much work it takes, it is important to form new habits and learn to live in love, understanding, and forgiveness. If counseling is necessary, then get Christian counseling.

As you know from reading my story, I also dealt with a serious case of rebellion. First Samuel 15:23 tells us that obedience is better than sacrifice; that rebellion is as the sin of witchcraft; and that stubbornness is as iniquity and idolatry. That scripture plainly tells me that as a Christian living in disobedience, rebellion, and stubbornness, I was no better off spiritually than I was as a sorcerer living in sin.

I mentioned earlier in the book that a demonic spirit actually mocked me after I ran from God and moved to New York. This spirit told me that he didn't have to leave my house because I was in rebellion. "You're no better than I am," the spirit informed me. At that point in my life, I was not a sorcerer; I had accepted Christ years earlier. And even though I was not demon possessed, I had lost my spiritual authority over the enemy because offense had caused me to fall into the sin of rebellion.

An attitude of rebellion often comes from past hurts. People say, "I've been hurt before and I'm not going to allow people to hurt me again. I'm going to be in charge now; I'm going to rule. Nobody can tell me what to do."

Sometimes people who have been abused by others will develop a rebellious spirit, which leads to a need to control others. This can also lead to a man or woman wanting every person of the opposite gender to pay for the way another man or woman treated them. Even a Christian who has been through a bad marriage or divorce can have a problem with this. People can be delivered from their rebellion and their need to control others, but oftentimes the problem stems from offense, anger, bitterness, and unforgiveness. Dealing with those issues and living in forgiveness are the first steps to receiving deliverance from a rebellious spirit.

We cannot take sin lightly. Today we don't hear much preaching about sin because some ministers fear it will offend people. But unrepentant sin is an open door to demonic oppression and possession. The Bible is very specific about the kinds of actions that are sinful. Let's start with something we're all familiar with: the Ten Commandments. They teach us to love and respect God, and to love and respect our fellow man. The first four commandments speak of how we are to treat God: We are not to live in idolatry by serving anything, anybody, or any god except Him; we must place Him first in our lives; we are not to take God's name in vain; and we are to keep the Sabbath day holy. The last six commandments tell us how to treat others: We are to honor our parents and never murder, commit adultery, steal, lie, or covet.

Galatians 5:19-21 lists the works of the flesh and tells us that people who practice these things will not inherit the kingdom of God. Ask yourself how many of these sinful works of the flesh you battle. These three verses read: "Now the works of the flesh are evident, which are adultery, fornication, uncleanness, lewdness, idolatry, sorcery, hatred, contentions, jealousies, outbursts of wrath, selfish ambitions, dissensions, heresies, envy, murders, drunkenness, revelries, and the like; of which I tell you beforehand, just as I also told you in time past, that those who practice such things will not inherit the kingdom of God."

The first sins mentioned are the sexual sins of adultery and fornication. The definition of fornication includes not only sexual relations outside of marriage, but also pornography, from which the Greek word for fornication is derived. Uncleanness refers to evil deeds and desires of the heart, while lewdness is following your passions to the point of having no shame. Revelry is excessive partying with alcohol, sex, drugs, and even food.

Idolatry is the worship of any god except the one true God. Idolatry doesn't refer only to false religions; you commit idolatry when you place anything or anybody above God. Sorcery and any kind of witchcraft, divination, or occult activity are also sin and idolatry.

Then there is murder and drunkenness. Maybe you're a good, church-going Christian who doesn't do any of those things. But what about the sins of hatred, envy, and jealousy? What about outbursts of explosive anger and rage? Galatians even lists contentions, which are quarrels or antagonism. And how many Christians are guilty of seeking power and having selfish ambitions?

Two sins mentioned that are often committed by religious people are dissensions and heresies. Dissensions are divisive teachings that are not supported by scripture, while heresies are erroneous opinions of man that are substituted for the truth of God's word.

Romans chapter one mentions those sins and several others: whisperers, backbiters, haters of God, the proud, and boasters. It speaks of those who practice deceit, those who are disobedient to parents, and those who are undiscerning, untrustworthy, unloving, and unmerciful.

That is a long list of sins, and that's not all of them. How many of us can honestly say that we never battle any of these sinful desires of human nature? Yet we must deal with our sins if we want to live a holy, sanctified, consecrated, and victorious life. Sin is a Christian's deadly enemy.

It is a shame that so many ministers would rather see their congregation spend eternity in hell than to risk their popularity by telling people they need to repent of their sinful lifestyles. In Second Timothy 4:2, the Apostle Paul told Timothy to reprove, rebuke, and exhort. He did not say, "Your job as a preacher is to make people feel good all the time." People's lives cannot be transformed unless they are willing to recognize their sin, repent, and learn to wage warfare over their weaknesses.

The Bible says that we must repent when we fall short. When we stop repenting and start allowing sin to rule, we open our lives to demonic spirits. If a Christian wants a demon, a Christian can have a demon.

When Christians become weak in their spiritual growth, they open the door for attack. It happens gradually. They stop praying and reading their Bible because they put other things ahead of spending time with God. They miss a few church services because there's something more important to do. They view an occasional movie or television program that they should not be watching. Maybe they look at pornography on the Internet. Then they help themselves to a girlfriend or boyfriend on the side.

Let's follow the path of destruction a little further. From pornography and adultery or fornication, a man continues in sin. He is never satisfied, so he wants a younger woman, then one who is even younger. Eventually he might become a pedophile and start having sexual relations with teenage girls. Maybe he will even molest children. The further he delves into sin, the less satisfied he is with that level of sin.

When evil spirits entice you to sin, they do not manifest themselves as something dark and evil. They pull you in slowly by making the sin look pleasurable and harmless. Once you are hooked, the enemy reels you in for the kill. When a husband and wife have an argument, the man storms off to work angry and another woman just happens to walk by and start a conversation. It seems innocent enough, but since the man is already angry with his wife, the enemy plants thoughts in his mind. *"This woman understands you so much better than your wife. You're a good-looking man; you could have any woman you wanted. You don't have to put up with somebody treating you the way your wife treats you."*

Before he knows what has happened, he has moved from talking to this woman to having a full-fledged affair. It was all a trick of the enemy to trap the man, break his marriage covenant, and lead him down a path to hell. And once the family is broken up, it becomes easier for the enemy to attack each person in the family.

This is not something you want to deal with. If you pray, fast, read your Bible, live a holy and obedient life, and are humble enough to repent when you sin, then you will not have to fear demonic spirits. Sure, they will attack you and try their best to influence you or tempt you to sin. Satan even tempted Jesus. But instead of giving in, Jesus quoted the Word of God and told Satan to flee. Thankfully, we can do the same. When the enemy comes knocking on your door, submit to God, resist the devil, and use your authority as a believer to make those evil spirits flee in the name of Jesus. Speak God's Word over your situation.

Conversely, if you don't get control of your sin when it is in the early stages, the sin will overtake you and your heart will become hardened. You will say, "I've been doing this for so long, why should I stop now?"

Unless we deal with all of our sins right away, we give the enemy a foothold. We open a door and give evil spirits permission to operate in our lives. From there we fall to another level of sin and still another level. In time we have committed a sin that causes us serious embarrassment. Deal with your sins now; lay aside every weight and every sin. After a while that sin will weigh you down and you won't want to get delivered.

When I preach like this, some ministers tell me that I am preaching too hard on sin. But I'm only telling people what the Bible says. When the church no longer thinks that sin is wrong, then it is the church that is wrong. Sometimes it is easier to shoot the messenger than to risk offending people by preaching against sin.

Anybody *can* sin and everybody *has* sinned. Many of us have a hall of shame. We all must deal with ours sins because sin alienates us from

God. It makes us morally and spiritually blind and causes us to become a slave to evil. When we sin, we cause innocent people to suffer. Sin brings guilt and condemnation; anxiety and distress; destruction and death. Sin causes us to become rebellious, idolatrous, arrogant, abusive, and corrupt. If we don't repent, we will find ourselves in hell for eternity.

James 1:14-15 says, "But each one is tempted when he is drawn away by his own desires and enticed. Then, when desire has conceived, it gives birth to sin; and sin, when it is full-grown, brings forth death." As Christians, we cannot tolerate sin; nor can we stop loving and praying for the sinner. The payment for sin is death, and we should do everything possible to keep our fellow man from dying a spiritual death. Jesus was crucified on the cross to save every sinner and to deliver them from every sin that keeps them in bondage. God is rich in mercy and, because of His great love, He will forgive us, save us by His grace, and make us alive together with Christ. It is the blood that Jesus shed on the cross that cleanses us from the sinful acts that lead to death.

Jesus taught that we should both repent and cast out the kingdom of darkness. If you are a believer in Christ who is living a holy life before God, there is no need to fear the enemy. Victory is yours; you have been given all authority over every demon in hell through God's Word and through the name and the blood of Jesus.

In Ephesians 6:10-18, the Apostle Paul tells us to be strong in the Lord and in the power of His might. He said, "Put on the whole armor of God, that you may be able to stand against the wiles of the devil. For we do not wrestle against flesh and blood, but against principalities, against powers, against the rulers of darkness of this age, against spiritual hosts of wickedness in the heavenly places." He told us to use the armor of God to fight the enemy and stand against the evil forces of hell. Our armor is faith, righteousness, truth, peace, salvation, the Word of God, and prayer—especially praying in the Spirit.

In recent years, Christians have been taught to ignore the devil and concentrate only on the Lord. Although I agree that we should concentrate on the Lord, I believe we have ignored the enemy to the point that we are ignorant of his devices. We can't understand why we struggle over and over with the same sins. We don't understand why we can't gain victory. We ignore the enemy, yet he doesn't go away. What is the problem?

A minister who has since gone home to be with the Lord once told me, "I don't want to be a fool. I want to learn the tricks of the enemy and be prepared. I don't want to fall for any of his tricks."

If we want victory over the enemy, we cannot be ignorant of his purposes and methods of attack. The Bible tells us that the whole world lies under the sway of the wicked one. What are we doing to allow his influence in our lives? If we lack knowledge, how can we recognize the source of the problem? How can we close the doors we have opened and keep them closed? How can we live in the victory that Jesus bought for us when He shed His blood and died on the cross?

The enemy is always crouching at your door, knocking to be let in. *Don't go to church today. You've had a rough week. Go to the lake instead... Why pray? God doesn't answer your prayers so don't even bother...Look what your husband did to you. Don't put up with that. You deserve better...It's just one little joint of marijuana. Go ahead; smoke it just this one time...It won't hurt to take a quick look at pornography. You can stop anytime you want.*

Recognize those thoughts as an ambush of the enemy. Replace those thoughts with the truth of God's word. Command the enemy to leave in the name of Jesus. Don't fall for any trap the enemy throws in your path to make you turn away from God. It is not a sin to be tempted; Hebrews

4:15 tells us that Jesus was tempted just as we are, yet He was without sin. Luke 4:13 records these words about the temptation of Jesus: "Now when the devil had ended every temptation, he departed from Him until an opportune time." Jesus spoke the Word of God over the temptation and told Satan to flee. Did he leave for good? Not according to this scripture. It tells us that Satan left for a while, but he came back later to try again.

Learning the tricks of the enemy is half the battle. Recognize his strategy and keep him under your feet. Stay in proper spiritual shape by living righteously, obediently, holy, and humbly before the Lord. Keep a repentant and forgiving heart; fast, pray, and stay in God's word. Keep yourself cleansed from all filthiness of the flesh and spirit, and remain holy in the fear of God. If you are living in this manner, you have all authority to follow the example of Jesus: quote the Word of God to Satan, and then command him to leave.

Believers need to stand and thrive in these days in which we are living. We need a bold faith. Jesus paid the price with His life to give us victory over the enemy, and we need to do everything possible to live in that victory. Don't be a slave to sin; allow God to set you free. There is enough power in the hem of His garment to give you the deliverance that you need and to set you free. And he whom the Son sets free is free indeed.

CHAPTER 14

Questions and Answers

"Even though we walk in the flesh, we do not war in the flesh. For the weapons of our warfare are not carnal but mighty in God for pulling down strongholds..."

- 2 Corinthians 10:3-4

I have never heard teaching like this before, and I'm not sure I believe that demonic spirits can cause the kinds of problems you mentioned. Is that biblical?

That's a valid question, because any kind of religious teaching should be backed up by scripture. Let's begin by looking at the ministry of Jesus and His disciples.

Mark 5:1-20 and Luke 8:26-39 record the story of Jesus casting demons out of a man who lived among the tombs. This man, who was possessed by at least two thousand demonic spirits, had supernatural strength and was able to break shackles and chains into pieces. Nobody could tame him. Demons had driven him into the wilderness. He lived in the mountains and the tombs, crying out and cutting himself. He wore no clothes. After Jesus told the unclean spirits to come out, the man was seen clothed and in his right mind.

Luke 13:10-17 tells of a woman who had a spirit of infirmity for eighteen years. She was bent over and could not raise herself up. When Jesus loosed this woman from the spirit of infirmity, her body immediately straightened up. Used in this context, infirmity means weakness, disease, sickness, lack of strength, or feebleness of body or mind. That definition covers a host of mental and physical ailments.

In Matthew 12:22, Jesus prayed for a blind and mute man who was demon-possessed, and the man both spoke and saw. Jesus cast a deaf and dumb spirit out of a boy, as recorded in Mark 9:14-29. This spirit sometimes caused him to have convulsions and seizures, and often it threw him into the fire or water in an attempt to kill him.

When Ananias and Sapphira lied, Peter asked, "Why has Satan filled your heart to lie to the Holy Spirit?" Here we see that the enemy puts it in our hearts to lie.

Jesus gave His disciples authority to drive out evil spirits and to heal every disease and sickness. Acts 5:16 tells us that people brought those who were sick and tormented by evil spirits, and all of them were healed. Acts 8:7 says that unclean spirits, crying with a loud voice, came out of many who were possessed. The Apostle Paul, in Acts 16:16, cast the demon out of a girl who was possessed by an evil spirit that caused her to predict the future.

This list is by no means all-inclusive; but in these verses alone, we can summarize some of the problems that demonic spirits can cause in the life of an individual. They cause supernatural strength, homelessness, mental anguish, cutting of the flesh, nakedness, weakness, sickness, disease, lack of strength, feebleness of body or mind, blindness, muteness, convulsions, seizures, suicide, lying, torment, and ability to predict the future through demonic methods.

My family has our own testimony about healing from the spirit of infirmity. When my son Christopher was about four years old, he was diagnosed with autism. Several doctors at university hospitals told us that he would never learn past a third grade level. Christopher wouldn't respond to any verbal commands, nor could he speak or otherwise communicate.

During one of his visits to a doctor's office, God spoke to me and said, "You are a deliverance minister. Don't accept the words of those doctors. You know how to cast out evil spirits, and you need to take authority over the spirits that are attacking your son's mind."

When God told me that, boldness came over me. I told the doctor that I was not going to accept the diagnosis that my son was autistic. I took my son by the hand, left the doctor's office, and took him home. I prayed, "I am not going to agree with what these doctors are saying. I am coming into agreement with the word of God. You evil spirit, I command you to leave my son right now in the name of Jesus. You are not getting my baby. The word of God says that he will have a sound mind. My son will be a man of knowledge and great understanding."

Christopher was healed, and he never had another problem with autism after God healed him. Today he is nineteen years old and has an intelligent, sound mind. He travels with me and is a tremendous help to me on the road.

Can just anybody cast out evil spirits?

Let me clearly emphasize that the answer to that question is no! You must be a born again believer in Christ, and you must be living righteously and without unrepentant sin.

Mark 16:17 says, "These signs will follow those who believe: In My name they will cast out demons…" And Luke 10:17-20 records the story of seventy people who returned after ministering in various cities. They were joyous that demonic spirits were subject to them in Jesus' name. But Jesus said to them, "Behold, I give you the authority to trample on serpents and scorpions, and over all the power of the enemy, and nothing shall by any means hurt you. Nevertheless do not rejoice in this, that the spirits are subject to you, but rather rejoice because your names are written in heaven."

There is a story in Acts 19:13-16 about a group of itinerant Jewish exorcists and the seven sons of a Jewish chief priest named Sceva who tried to cast out evil spirits by saying, "We exorcise you by the Jesus whom Paul preaches."

An evil spirit answered, "Jesus I know, and Paul I know, but who are you?"

Then the man who was possessed by the evil spirit leaped on the men, overpowered them, and prevailed against them. The Bible says the men fled from the house naked and wounded.

If you are not a believer, or if you accepted Christ but are living with unrepentant sin, do not try casting out demons at home or anywhere else. You might end up like the seven sons of Sceva.

Even if you are a believer, please do not get motivated in the flesh to cast demonic spirits out of every person who appears to be demon possessed. Use wisdom. If the Holy Spirit is not leading you to perform deliverance on somebody, don't do it.

When it comes to deliverance, always start by cleaning up your own life and taking authority over your own problems. Deal with your own household first. Then with prayer and fasting, and as you are led by the Holy Spirit, deal with demonic strongholds in the lives of others that God places in your path.

Is it possible for demonic spirits to remain in a house after the residents have moved out?

Absolutely. You never know what kind of evil activities occurred in that house or apartment before you moved in. The previous residents could have been involved in all kinds of illegal, immoral, or occultist activity. Demonic spirits take up residence in those places. I pity the people who moved into our home in Stamford, Connecticut after our dad left.

When you move into a house, immediately take authority over any spirits that might have taken up residence. Speak blessings and the blood of Jesus over the home, your possessions, and your family. Even in a newly built home, you never know what might have happened in years past on the land where the home sits. As a child of God, you should never allow demonic spirits to stay in your home and torment you.

A friend of mine bought a house in Beverly Hills that was previously owned by an actor who was involved in the occult. After my friend moved into the house, his children were tormented every night. It didn't matter that the bedrooms were gorgeous and the house was worth several million dollars. Evil spirits had taken over.

The parents finally called me to come check it out. As soon as I walked in the house, I knew what had been going on before they moved in. The waster spirit even started to materialize in front of my eyes. I said, "I knew you were here. You can't hide from me because I know who you are."

We took anointing oil, prayed the Word of God over the house, and commanded the evil spirits to leave in the name of Jesus. We prayed in our prayer language of the Holy Spirit as we walked throughout the house. Those demonic spirits were forced to flee. From that moment on, the children never had another problem with tormenting spirits.

If you find that you are dealing with tormenting spirits in your home; if you or your children are becoming fearful or skittish; or if you are hearing sounds of a haunted house, start praying and commanding those spirits to leave in the name of Jesus. Ask some saints of God to come to your home and have a prayer meeting. You must take authority over these spirits if you want to have peace in your home.

When I travel, I sometimes sense an evil presence in the hotel rooms where I'm staying. Is there something I can do about this?

Indeed there is. Pray when you get into that hotel room and command every evil spirit to leave in the name of Jesus. Pray that the blood of Jesus and the peace of God will cover your room. If you are a Holy Spirit-filled believer, pray in your prayer language. Some people play praise and worship music in the hotel rooms where they stay. Your objective is to change the atmosphere in the room, and this is how you do it.

I find that I must pray over every hotel room where I stay. All kinds of things may have occurred in that room, and changing the sheets does not change the spirits.

One time a pastor invited me to speak at his church. I was getting ready to preach about one topic when the Holy Spirit said to me, "Stop. Talk about cigarettes. There are people here who love me, but they still smoke. They need deliverance."

So I preached on deliverance from cigarettes. People all over the chapel came forward and threw their cigarettes on the altar. The pharmakeia spirit that keeps people on drugs is the same spirit that keeps them addicted to nicotine. When people get delivered from their nicotine habit, you can see the difference in their countenance.

After the service, my son Christopher and I returned to our hotel room. That night I was attacked in my room by evil spirits. One spirit said to me, "How dare you take my people from me! I'm going to take all your strength from you."

I am six foot five, but this spirit towered over me and picked me up. I heard the Lord say, "Don't panic. Plead the blood."

The evil spirit was still holding me as I said, "Get your hands off me! I command you to leave me alone in the name of Jesus. I plead the blood of Jesus. Let me go in the name of Jesus!"

"Don't say that!" the spirit ordered. With that, he released me and fled. I was thanking Jesus when two more spirits came out of the floor. I heard the Lord say, "Don't panic. What did you do with the last one?"

Again I said, "Get out of here in the name of Jesus. I plead the blood of Jesus; I plead the blood of Jesus!" The spirits disappeared. They hate to hear mention of the name and the blood of Jesus; at that name, they have to flee.

After they were gone, I lay in bed thinking to myself, "If these things get so upset over cigarettes, imagine how upset they must be when somebody gets delivered from something really bad." But the fact is that it doesn't matter what people are getting delivered from. The enemy wants to control everything—including cigarettes.

I have also had demonic spirits appear in my hotel room and tell me that they are going to kill me. Evil spirits are gifted at making a nuisance of themselves. But if you are a child of God whose name is written in the Lamb's Book of Life, simply command them to flee in the name of Jesus and cover the room with the protection of the blood of Jesus.

I am a born-again believer in Christ, but when I try to pray, I often cannot concentrate on what I'm saying long enough to get a prayer through. My mind wanders and I think about everything except prayer. Why does this happen and what can I do about it?

There is a blockade spirit that stands over us at times when we pray. Witches call it the one-eyed, one-armed blockade spirit. It will even put its arm around you and try to pull you up from off your knees. I can assure you that you have felt its presence at some point. This is the spirit that brings all kinds of things to your mind while you pray. Try as you might, instead of praying, you will find yourself thinking about an item you left off your grocery list, your car's faulty transmission, the horn blowing outside your house, and a hundred other things.

This spirit blocks communication between you and heaven by using thoughts of your everyday life. Instead of concentrating on prayer, the focus becomes on life, worry, and uncertainty, which can lead to doubt and fear. Even doubt and fear are attacks of the enemy.

A blockade spirit will also whisper things to you about your past in an effort to hinder your prayer life. You will feel that you don't deserve anything from God, so why ask.

The enemy is also capable of blocking the answer to your prayers, as we see in Daniel chapter ten. For three weeks Daniel fasted and prayed, until at last a messenger was sent from God to tell Daniel, "From the first day that you set your heart to understand and to humble yourself before your God, your words were heard; and I have come because of your words. But the prince of the kingdom of Persia withstood me twenty-one days; and behold, Michael, one of the chief princes, came to help me, for I had been left alone there with the kings of Persia."

In this example, God heard Daniel's prayers from the moment he prayed. But the answer took twenty-one days because of an unseen spiritual battle that was being waged in the heavenly atmosphere.

What should you do when you have problems praying because you cannot concentrate on prayer and the enemy constantly brings other things to mind? You are a child of God, so simply say, "In the name of Jesus, I command every foul spirit to leave this room. I am going to pray, and my prayers will not be blocked. They will get through and be answered." Then press through in prayer.

Before you pray, it helps to first read scripture, listen to worship music, and spend time praising and thanking God. Create an atmosphere of true worship as you enter God's presence.

We are experiencing terrible division in our church right now. It seems like we are on the verge of split right down the middle. I know this is a spiritual battle, but what exactly are we dealing with?

Most likely you are dealing with the wedge fox, a spirit that is mentioned in Luke 13:32 when Jesus said to the Pharisees, "Go tell that fox, 'Behold, I cast out demons and perform cures today and tomorrow…' "

The Herodians were a group of influential pro-Roman Pharisees who tried to divide the Jews. Even though they didn't like Jesus, they told him in Luke 13:31 to leave town because Herod wanted to kill him.

When Jesus responded by saying, "Go tell that fox…," someone reading that might think that Jesus was metaphorically calling Herod a fox. But I saw that differently. I saw that Jesus was calling the spirit a fox. Jesus wasn't saying, "Go tell that fox Herod that I cast out demons." He was saying, "Go tell that evil fox spirit that I cast out demons."

In witchcraft, this spirit is called a wedge fox because it drives a wedge between people—between friends, family members, business partners, church members, deacons and the pastor, choir members and the choir director, and so forth. It particularly goes after those who are in positions of authority. The wedge fox is a spirit that causes division.

Every occult practitioner knows about this spirit. I knew about it from my sorcery days; in fact, when I wanted to break up something, I sent a fox spirit to cause division. This works especially well when there is already a problem brewing. It's easier to tear something down when it is weak to begin with. After I became a believer, I was shocked to see this spirit mentioned in the Bible.

I dare say that almost every church split was caused by a fox spirit that nobody recognized or took authority over. Many times the problems start over little things. Song of Solomon 2:15 tells us that little foxes spoil the vine. There could be many little foxes in homes and churches that cause division and problems between people. And instead of fighting the spirit, people fight each other. Let's say there is a disagreement between a leader and somebody with less authority. The leader might say, "If you don't like it, why don't you leave?" Instead of resolving their problems in a biblical fashion, they devour each other.

Why do you think we have so many denominations? It's because people fought and divided over issues like water baptism or speaking in tongues. Why do you think we have black churches and white churches? It's because of the wedge fox spirit that comes to bring division. Again, use your authority as a believer to command it to leave in the name of Jesus. Don't let this spirit disrupt your family, your choir, your church, or anything else.

There are other spirits that attack churches; for example, there is a dispatching spirit that works like a taxi service that dispatches cars to pick up riders. The purpose of a dispatching spirit is to take over and destroy a church. For example, it might send a jezebel spirit or a charlatan spirit to attack the church.

A church must be covered in prayer, from the leadership on down. Fasting should occur on a regular basis, again from the leadership on down. If you are having problems in your church, ask God to reveal to you the spirit behind the attacks. He might even show you a visible manifestation of the spirit, so be prepared for what you might see. Speak the Word of God over the situation, take authority over the spirit, and command it to leave in Jesus' name.

The problem of our young people cutting their flesh has become prevalent in our society today. What is behind that?

Indeed, there are many young people today who engage in the practice of using a knife to cut their flesh. Some say they do it to see if they are alive. Others say they do it to relieve the pain in their lives.

Any young person who cuts their flesh is suffering from the effects of tormenting demonic spirits. Much of what happens in the demonic realm involves the shedding of blood—especially the shedding of innocent blood. Just as our blameless Lord and Savior Jesus Christ shed His blood for us as a sacrifice, the enemy wants a blood sacrifice, too. And one way he gets it is to convince people to cut their own flesh to draw blood. He wants people who were created by God and in God's image to inflict pain upon themselves.

In Leviticus and Deuteronomy, God specifically prohibited tattooing and cutting. In Leviticus 19:28, God told the Israelites, *"You shall not make any cuttings in your flesh for the dead, nor tattoo any marks upon you."* In those days, pagan cults tattooed their followers while mourning their dead. Tattooing and cutting were a custom among savage tribes, and this practice is still seen in some parts of the world today.

Tattooing and cutting were prohibited by God for two reasons: both were used by pagans for idolatrous purposes; and God taught His people to respect and revere His creation. They were not permitted to unnaturally disfigure their bodies.

In scripture, before Elijah called fire down on the altar, the priests of Baal danced around their own altar and cut themselves with lances and knives until their blood gushed. The Carians cut their foreheads with knives at the festival of their god Isis, and Syrian priests cut their arms and tongues with swords. Since there are no new tricks in the devil's book, it should be no surprise that the enemy still convinces people to cut themselves.

The answer for those who cut their flesh is salvation through Christ Jesus. Only He can bring freedom and deliverance to their hurting souls. Without Jesus, psychiatric counseling is only a temporary fix. Of course the root cause of the hurt must be identified, because dealing with that root cause will help close the door that was opened to the enemy. For example, has the young person been sexually abused or abandoned by a parent? If so, emotional pain has likely led to anger, bitterness, and unforgiveness. Even after the young person comes to Christ, it is important to deal with the root issue. They should repent of their unforgiveness and ask God to remove the bitterness from their heart.

Young people today are forced to deal with issues that many parents could have never imagined when they were growing up. We should not assume that problems such as cutting are an attempt to gain attention. Instead, we should see those problems as a cry of pain. The enemy wants to control our children so he can destroy their lives. As believers, we cannot allow that to happen.

My church hired a magician to perform at a special event. Is it okay for someone to perform magic tricks in church?

Not in any church that I pastor. I once visited a church in a southern state and was shocked to see magicians performing there. Coming from a witchcraft and voodoo background, I was very upset to see these people coming into the church to perform magic. There were children sitting in the front row. And believe me, these children will remember that, and some will want to be a magician when they grow up.

There is an evil spirit that assists a magician during a magic trick. It will, for example, hand the magician all of those things he is pulling out of a hat. In the meantime, everybody in the audience is oohing and aah-ing over the antics of a demonic spirit.

Magic once flourished in Egypt and other Middle-Eastern cultures. In the seventh chapter of Exodus, when Pharaoh refused to let the chil-dren of Israel leave Egypt, God brought plagues against the nation. As God supernaturally brought the plagues, Pharaoh called forth his own magicians and sorcerers. Worshippers of Egypt's many gods believed they had the power to send their gods forth to perform on their behalf. When God sent a plague of frogs, for example, the magicians brought even more frogs upon the land, just to prove that their gods could also call forth frogs.

The signs and wonders that were performed by God against the Egyp-tians affected the things in nature that the Egyptians worshipped, such as the Nile River, the sun, a god that was represented by a frog's head, and even flies. To see plagues brought against the things that represented their gods must have been humiliating to the Egyptians.

To those who don't have a background in the occult, I'm sure I sound alarmist when I oppose "simple" magic tricks. But with my years of voo-doo training, I know the dangers of magic, witchcraft, divination, slight of hand, and illusion. It doesn't matter what you call it. It's still forbidden by God and it's very dangerous to dabble in it.

I've had five abortions. Will God forgive me for what I have done to the unborn children I carried?

If you ask Him to forgive you, He will. You must also forgive your-self. When I had my near-death experience in the hospital and went to paradise, I saw children who had been aborted. So I know that aborted children are with the Lord in heaven.

Once you have repented and sought Christ's forgiveness, He forgives you and blots out your past. You must then walk in His forgiveness by moving forward with your life and not allowing the enemy to keep bringing up your past. Instead, allow God to use for good what the enemy meant for evil. In your case, you can use your experiences and the knowledge you have gained to keep other people from making the same mistake. You might consider volunteering your time at a crisis pregnancy or adoption center.

Is it possible for me to stop lusting? Every time a nice-looking girl walks by I lust. How can I overcome this?

When dealing with lust or any other temptation, our greatest weapon is the word of God. Know what the Bible says and use those scriptures to fight the enemy. The Apostle Paul wrote in Ephesians chapter 6 about the importance of putting on the whole armor of God so that we can stand against the schemes of the enemy.

James 1:14 says that a man is tempted when he is drawn away by his own lusts and enticed. God gave us His word and other weapons to fight temptation and overcome lust of the flesh. First Corinthians 10:13 tells us, "No temptation has overtaken you except such as is common to man; but God is faithful, who will not allow you to be tempted beyond what you are able, but with the temptation will also make the way of escape, that you may be able to bear it." If you find yourself in situations that cause you to be tempted, stay away from those situations.

Galatians 5:16 tells us, "Walk in the Spirit, and you shall not fulfill the lust of the flesh." Determine in your heart that you will begin to exercise self-control, which is a fruit of the Spirit. Look only upon those things that are honoring to God. Job had the right idea when he made a covenant with his eyes that he would not look upon a woman lustfully.

It is not a sin to be tempted, but it is a sin to act on the temptation. Jesus responded to Satan's temptations by quoting God's written word. Satan fled, but Luke told us that he left until an opportune time, meaning that Satan's last thoughts were along the lines of, "I'll be back."

Even though we might resist temptation this time, the devil doesn't give up. He will return to try again. Resist him and keep quoting the word of God over your situation. Ask God to help you commit yourself to holiness. If you put on your spiritual armor and get yourself in top condition through prayer, fasting, and regular Bible reading, temptation and lust can be dealt with.

What causes me to choke at night? Sometimes it seems like there's something standing over me and choking me.

There is a spirit called pavor nocturnus that Haitian voodoo practitioners call forth when they want to kill people—business competitors, for example. This spirit will choke people at night, and it also causes sudden infant death syndrome. It will choke a person by using its oversized hands, by using a rope, or by suffocating the person with its wings.

How do you deal with this? Don't go to bed without praying. Pray over your babies before you put them to bed. Don't let a night go by without praying for God's protection over your family and home.

I recall hearing about a hotel in Japan that was closed down because several men who were guests in the hotel died in their sleep one night. There was no clue as to what caused their deaths; but more than likely it was this spirit that choked or suffocated them.

I sometimes experience pain in my body but the doctors can't find anything wrong. Could this be some kind of demonic attack?

It could indeed. There is a phantom pain spirit that attacks people, usually as a piercing or stabbing pain. Doctors will never find a cause when people are experiencing pain caused by this spirit.

This is the same spirit that attacks when sorcerers use voodoo dolls. These dolls are still used in certain countries, as well as cities in America where voodoo is practiced, such as New Orleans and New York City. I am not saying that if you have phantom pain that it means you are experiencing a voodoo attack. I'm simply saying that it is the same spirit.

One purpose of this attack is to control your mind by trapping you into taking pain medication or sedatives, to which you can become addicted. Sorcery and drugs are directly connected, as I learned from my years of training. The sorcerer speaks incantations over the drugs before they are administered, and the goal is to control people through the use of the drugs. The job of the pharmakeia spirit is to get people addicted to various kinds of drugs, both legal and illegal.

Please understand that I am not telling you to stop taking your prescribed medications, but I do believe that you should seek the face of God about the medications you are taking. With my background and knowledge, I personally am opposed to most drugs, and especially any medication to which someone might become addicted. The pharmakeia spirit has taken over American society, and our answer to every problem seems to be a drug.

If you are a child of God who is experiencing pain for which the doctors can offer no explanation, lay your hand on the spot where you have the pain and say something like, "I come against this phantom pain spirit and command it to leave in the name of Jesus. I am a child of God and you are no longer permitted to attack my body. Jesus defeated you at the cross and He bore all of my infirmities. I pray the promise of God over myself and say that no weapon formed against me will prosper."

While it is certainly possible that you have a medical condition that has not yet been diagnosed, if you are a believer who is experiencing an attack of the enemy, this prayer will work.

I don't understand what is wrong with certain things that some people consider occultist. What is wrong with reading my horoscope? Or having a psychic reading? Isn't that just harmless fun?

These things might seem like harmless fun; but by dabbling in *anything* related to the occult, you are opening the door to demonic influence and attack in your life. You might think you are engaging in harmless fun, but the devil always plays for keeps.

All of these things are forbidden in the Bible because they are pagan and demonic. Here is what Deuteronomy 18:10-11 tells us: "There shall not be found among you anyone who makes his son or his daughter pass through the fire, or one who practices witchcraft, or a soothsayer, or one who interprets omens, or a sorcerer, or one who conjures spells, or a medium, or a spiritist, or one who calls up the dead. For all who do these things are an abomination to the Lord, and because of these abominations the Lord your God drives them out from before you."

Passing a son or daughter through the fire refers to the practice of child sacrifice. To appease their pagan gods, people sacrificed their children by throwing them into the fiery belly of a god named Molech. A comparable action today is abortion.

Witchcraft includes those things that some consider harmless—even white witchcraft or Wicca. It doesn't matter what you call it. God still forbids it. And sorcery, even though it was practiced by some of Israel's wicked kings, is forbidden as well.

Soothsayers were people who read the clouds or heavenly bodies, which is similar to astrology or tea leaf reading of today. Soothsayers (also called diviners) were pagan counterparts to the biblical prophets. Divination is an attempt to see into the future through demonic means, while biblical prophecy is divinely inspired by God.

Practices that involved superstition were also forbidden in the Bible. There are two unusual and forbidden practices of divination mentioned that were forms of superstition. Ezekiel 21:21 mentions reading the livers of sacrificial animals, as well as throwing down arrows to see which route is the will of their pagan god.

Conjuring spells, consulting mediums, performing séances and calling up the dead, telling fortunes (and having your fortune told), and performing incantations or magic rituals that enlist demonic spirits are all forbidden.

All of these practices are controlled by evil spirits, and God doesn't want His people to be involved with anything evil. Why dabble in the occult when you know it is a sin that opens the door for an attack by the enemy?

It seems that so many people today, even many Christians, center their focus on money and material possessions. I don't have a problem believing that God wants to bless His children. But what causes people to become so greedy and obsessed with money and material things?

In Matthew 6:24 the Bible says, "No one can serve two masters; for either he will hate one and love the other, or else he will be loyal to the one and despise the other. You cannot serve God and mammon." Mammon is a word for wealth and riches. But there is an evil spirit that considers itself mammon.

When I was eleven years old, the pillardoc spirit offered me the opportunity to become a bank robber, much like my idol at that time, Willie Sutton. This spirit said, "I make one person rich and another person poor. Some see me as mammon. Don't trust God. Trust me."

This spirit will cause a person to become so greedy that they want more and more money, even when they already have so much that they will never be able to spend it in a lifetime. Conversely, it will cause people to lose whatever money they might have, or get fired from every job they work.

Poverty is caused by this spirit, and it will attach itself to families for generations. It will cause people to worry over money to the point that they become physically ill or even commit suicide.

Zapan is the primary spirit behind arson, but pillardoc also causes people to become so frustrated over their financial situation that they burn down their business or their house just to get insurance money. It will cause people to murder a family member for the insurance money.

This spirit told me to follow him and I would be rich. Although I never robbed banks, I still followed the directions of evil spirits. And there was a time in my early years when I was making more money in one day than most grown men made in one week. I had so much money that I sometimes threw dollar bills away.

I certainly do not believe that God wants His people to be poor, but neither does He want us to be greedy and chase after money. First Timothy 6:10 tells us, "For the love of money is the root of all kinds of evil, for which some have strayed from the faith in their greediness, and pierced themselves through with many sorrows."

God is our provider and we need to serve Him, not mammon. We also need to remember the words of Matthew 6:19-21: "Do not lay up for yourselves treasures on earth, where moth and rust destroy and where thieves break in and steal. But lay up for yourselves treasures in heaven, where neither moth nor rust destroys and where thieves do not break in and steal. For where your treasure is, there your heart will be also."

An acquaintance of mine often makes comments about other people that I find disturbing. For example, she might say, "I wish something would happen to teach him a lesson." What can I say to help her understand that she shouldn't say those things?

When someone speaks this way, it is called wishcraft, and it is a low form of witchcraft. When you say that somebody makes you sick, you might just get sick. When you say that you wish something would happen to teach someone a lesson, you are cursing that individual. We cannot make the curse less effective by laughing about it or pretending it was a joke.

Chapter three of the book of James talks about the untamable tongue, and the first twelve verses are very important. We are told that the tongue defiles the whole body, and with it we curse men who have been made in the likeness of God. Out of the same mouth come blessings and curses, and that should not be.

People often say things that they don't realize are a form of witchcraft. They might say, "I can't stand that guy. I wish he'd drop dead." Instead of praying over a person, which is what we are supposed to do, curses are spoken over the person. And by doing so, you are inviting demonic spirits to attack the person. This is a terrible thing to do, and it should never happen.

We must learn to watch the words we speak. Here is another example. There are plenty of former drug addicts, alcoholics, and prison inmates who are saved, delivered, and preaching the Gospel. They were delivered and saved by the blood of Jesus, and He is going to keep them delivered. These people don't say, "I'm a recovering alcoholic, and I know that I could fall off the wagon and go back anytime." If you speak like that, you increase the likelihood that you will revert to your sinful ways.

Someone who has been delivered by the power of God should simply say, "Praise God, I'm delivered. And I don't ever intend to go back to what the Lord delivered me from!" Don't confess that you will always be an alcoholic or a drug addict. When God delivers you, He sets you free from those bondages of sin. The devil is not more powerful than Jesus Christ and His shed blood.

After years of denial, I finally recognize that I am having a problem with unforgiveness. What can you tell me that will help me overcome this battle?

One of the greatest weapons of the enemy is offense. If Satan can convince us that we have a right to be offended, then he can easily keep us in bondage. Offense causes us to hold a grudge, which makes us angry and bitter. Anger and bitterness lead to unforgiveness, which causes us to hold on to the belief that we have a right to feel the way we do because of how we were treated. We might spend our lives wanting to make the person pay for what they did to us.

Once we convince ourselves that we have a right to live with unforgiveness, all kinds of things can happen. Unforgiveness severs our link to God and hinders our prayer life. Our negative attitude will affect our relationship with others. Our health will be destroyed as we develop a multitude of physical and mental disorders, including stress-related illnesses and depression. The physical and mental effects of bitterness and unforgiveness have been medically well-documented. And as long as you are living with bitterness and unforgiveness, you can pray all the prayers you want and you will not be healed.

The person against whom we are holding the grudge might have gone on with their life and forgotten all about the incident. They might not recognize you if they passed you in the grocery store. And sometimes the person we haven't forgiven was buried in the ground a long time ago.

I know what it is like to deal with unforgiveness, because I dealt with rage for ten years after I accepted Christ. My rage was a result of unforgiveness over the things my father did to me when I was growing up. One time I was helping Kenneth and Gloria Copeland, and Kenneth sensed something and asked me what was wrong. I explained to him that, even though I was saved and filled with the Holy Spirit, I still could not get out of my head the things my father had done to me. They both said, "Earthquake, until you get that out of your mind and forgive your father, you will never be the man of God that He called you to be."

I went back to my hotel room and got on my knees. I repented and asked God to take that bitterness and unforgiveness from me. And that is exactly what God did. I released my father from the unforgiveness I held for all those years, and I was free. I'm thankful that the Copeland's were bold enough to tell me the truth.

Years later, I became bitter over a handful of ministers who fought my deliverance message, and that led me into rebellion. Do you see how the enemy works? God was not going to move on my behalf as long as I lived with anger, bitterness, and rebellion.

Let's look at what the Bible says about unforgiveness. In Colossians 3:12-13 we find this verse: "Therefore, as the elect of God, holy and beloved, put on tender mercies, kindness, humility, meekness, longsuffering; bearing with one another, and forgiving one another, if anyone has a complaint against another; even as Christ forgave you, so you also must do." These verses tell us that we should have patience and mercy in dealing with the frailties of other people, and that we must forgive others, just as Christ forgave us.

Part of the Lord's Prayer in Matthew 6:12 says, "Forgive us our trespasses as we forgive those who trespass against us." In verses 14 and 15, we read some frightening words that were spoken by Jesus Himself: "For if you forgive men their trespasses, your heavenly Father will also forgive you. But if you do not forgive men their trespasses, neither will your Father forgive your trespasses." We can sugarcoat those verses and look for loopholes all we want, but the fact remains that Jesus is telling us that we have to forgive those who wronged us if we expect God to forgive us.

Jesus told a story in Matthew chapter 18 that we call "the parable of the unforgiving servant." There was a king who wanted to settle accounts with his servants. One of those servants owed a tremendous debt that he could never repay. The king showed him mercy and compassion and forgave the entire debt.

But when that same forgiven servant found one of his own fellow servants who owed him a small amount of money, he threw the man in prison until he could repay the debt. When the king learned what happened, he became angry and delivered the forgiven servant unto the torturers until he could repay his own debt (which, of course, was a debt that he could never repay).

This parable ends with a warning from Jesus: "So My heavenly Father also will do to you if each of you, from his heart, does not forgive his brother his trespasses."

We need to take this issue of unforgiveness seriously. Our Lord and Savior Jesus Christ was blameless and sinless, yet He carried all of our sins and died on a cross so that we could be free of a debt we could never repay. When we accept His gift of salvation, we are forgiven unconditionally. He forgets our sins and never brings them up again. How then can we, in our pride and arrogance, think that we have a right to live in unforgiveness toward somebody who wronged us?

Until you forgive, no matter how terrible the act committed against you, the joy of the Lord will not operate in your life. Even though my dad taught me voodoo, ruined my childhood, and beat me severely in the head, I still had to forgive him. Anything less than complete forgiveness is an open door to the enemy.

The Apostle Paul said that he forgave, "lest Satan should take advantage of us, for we are not ignorant of his devices." Offense is one of Satan's devices to keep you from living in the freedom and abundance that Jesus offered you when He died on the cross.

Once we understand that we are not dealing with flesh and blood, but with demonic powers that control and influence people, it becomes easier to see others as people who were created by God and in God's image. We see them as people who have allowed the enemy too much control in their lives, just as you are doing when you live with bitterness and unforgiveness.

If we interpret the scriptures on unforgiveness literally, we have to realize that unforgiveness could keep us out of heaven. When we know what God's word says and we still disobey Him, we are telling Him, "I don't care what you say. I'm not going to forgive because I have a right to feel this way after what this person did to me." That attitude is nothing more than rebellion toward God. Rebellion is as the sin of witchcraft, and rebellion will keep you out of heaven.

Don't take a chance by letting the enemy get the upper hand in your life. Forgive those who have wronged you and release the ball and chain you have been dragging around all those years.

Is there anything wrong with telling a "little white lie?"

It is not okay to lie, even a little bit. God hates liars, and the Bible tells us in Revelation 21:8, "But the cowardly, unbelieving, abominable, murderers, sexually immoral, sorcerers, idolaters, and all liars shall have their part in the lake which burns with fire and brimstone, which is the second death." No special provision was made in that verse—or anywhere else in the Bible—for people who tell little white lies to keep themselves out of trouble.

Even Christians have a tendency to tell little lies. But a little white lie is witchcraft. White lies come from the mouths of witches who try to manipulate a situation to their advantage. When we tell a lie—even a little one—we are trying to manipulate or save our hide and get ourselves out of a sticky situation. Sometimes people even wink as they tell the lie, and that is deception. All of this is sin, and it comes from the enemy. At the end of the day, look back and ask yourself how many lies you told. You might be shocked.

One of my relatives used her children as mediums when she "contacted the dead." Now her children are adults and their lives are a wreck. They have never accepted Christ, and it is impossible to talk to them about Jesus. I don't want to see them die lost, but the situation seems hopeless. What can I do?

First, I want to make sure that the people reading this understand that your relative was not contacting the dead, nor were the dead speaking through her children. Your relative was calling forth familiar spirits that pretended to be the deceased person. That practice is evil and demonic, and it is specifically forbidden in scripture.

The children became possessed by demonic spirits as a result of being used as mediums by their mother. That is a tragedy indeed. The reason it is impossible for you to talk to your relatives about a relationship with Christ is because they are so bound by demonic spirits that the spirits do not want them to respond to your efforts. But don't stop trying! Keep praying for them and telling them about the deliverance that is available through Jesus Christ.

In this situation, you are dealing with evil spirits that have been tormenting these people for years. Spend time in fasting and serious prayer for their salvation and deliverance; fasting and prayer are two powerful weapons. Once you are in proper spiritual condition, and as you are led by the Holy Spirit, tell them that you are going to pray for their deliverance. Lay hands on each of your relatives and command the evil spirits to come out in the name of Jesus. Lead your relatives in a prayer of salvation, where they confess that Jesus is their Saviour and Lord; that they are delivered by the blood of Jesus; that they renounce their involvement in the occult; and that the evil spirits must flee and never return.

The tragedy of this kind of situation is that people who are this bound by demonic spirits cannot be helped by most Christians since many lack the simple knowledge to help these people. I have even heard pastors tell those who are seeking deliverance that the church can't help them. "You're on your own," they say.

Sitting in the pews of every church are people who are living in bondage and need deliverance. How can people who are in bondage help others who are in bondage? And how will people ever receive deliverance if the church can't help them?

Does hell really exist?

You bet it does. I've been to hell; and I can tell you from personal experience that hell is a lonely place of sorrow and constant torment. I had no control over anything, and there was nothing I could do to stop the torment. Evil spirits mocked and cursed me, bit and hit me, and pulled at my flesh. Their hands felt like knives piercing my body. They beat and twisted my head. There were even small demonic spirits inside my mouth. The horror was unspeakable. In hell, I was trapped and without hope. All the things I had ever done wrong came to mind. I have heard the agonizing screams of people pleading for a second chance.

You don't want to go to this place of torment and I don't want to go back. God doesn't want any of us to go there, either. That is why He gave us a multitude of warnings throughout the Bible about hell and the final judgment. But many people—even those in the church—scoff at His warnings. Perhaps that is why God allows people to experience hell and come back to give others a warning.

Dr. Maurice Rawlings, a retired cardiologist residing in Chattanooga, Tennessee, has written books about heaven and hell after resuscitating people who died and personally entered one destination or the other. He interviewed many of his patients and wrote of their near-death experiences. He once stated that he never met anybody who experienced hell who didn't come to a relationship with Christ after being resuscitated.

There are many biblical references to hell, some of which are listed in the study guide at the back of this book. Here are just three of those references:

"The wicked shall be turned into hell, and all the nations that forget God" (Psalm 9:17).

"Do not fear those who kill the body but cannot kill the soul. But rather fear Him who is able to destroy both soul and body in hell" (Matthew 10:28).

"And I saw the dead, small and great, standing before God, and books were opened. And another book was opened, which is the Book of Life. And the dead were judged according to their works, by the things which were written in the books. The sea gave up the dead who were in it, and death and hell delivered up the dead who were in them. And they were judged, each one according to his works. Then death and hell were cast into the lake of fire. This is the second death. And anyone not found written in the Book of Life was cast into the lake of fire" (Revelation 20:12-15).

There are plenty of scoffers and false teachers on earth today who don't believe that hell exists; who don't believe that people go there; or who don't believe that a person can experience hell and return to tell about it. Religious scoffers existed in Jesus' day, too. Remember the Pharisees, scribes, and Sadducees? If Jesus Himself was ridiculed and persecuted, then why should we expect anything less?

It isn't popular to preach about hell. Many ministers are afraid that people will be offended if they are told that they must repent of their sins or face eternity in hell. I agree that the way to reach people is not to bash them over the head with an angry fire and brimstone message. But instead of being balanced with the message, the enemy has made ministers so fearful of mentioning hell that they have gone to the other extreme. It seems that many are more afraid of mentioning hell than they are of going there.

There is proof in the Bible that many people who think they are going to heaven will end up in hell. Matthew 7:21-23 tells us, "Not everyone who says to Me, 'Lord, Lord,' shall enter the kingdom of heaven, but he who does the will of my Father in heaven. Many will say to Me in that day, 'Lord, Lord, have we not prophesied in Your name, cast out demons in Your name, and done many wonders in Your name?' And then I will declare to them, 'I never knew you; depart from Me, you who practice lawlessness!' "

Because of today's politically correct mindset, there are people sitting in our churches who believe they will go to heaven when they die. But if they die in their current spiritual condition, they will find themselves in hell. God did not say that joining a church, attending a church, or being baptized guarantees your entrance to heaven. You get to heaven by repenting of your sins and living a holy life.

Two years before dying at the age of fifteen and going to hell, I had been in church and given my life to Christ. Decades later, I considered myself a good Christian when I died in the emergency room and felt myself falling into hell. That time, God allowed me to hear the cries and the agony of people who considered themselves Christians, yet died in their rebellion and found themselves in hell.

If you want biblical proof that rebellious people go to hell, read the story of Jonah. God told Jonah to go to the wicked city of Nineveh and preach, but instead of obeying, he ran. Circumstances caused Jonah to be thrown out of a boat during a storm, and a great fish swallowed him. You've been told since you were a child that Jonah survived in the belly of the fish for three days. But if you read the second chapter of the book of Jonah carefully, it appears that Jonah drowned and went to Sheol (hell). Biblical scholars disagree over whether he was actually in hell or simply at the gates of hell, but most agree that it was one or the other.

After three days, God brought Jonah back to life. His spirit entered his dead body—which God had protected inside the belly of a fish— and the fish spat Jonah onto dry land. After that experience, Jonah had no problem obeying God and preaching in Nineveh. As a result of Jonah's obedience, the people of Nineveh repented and God spared the city from destruction. Do you see why we must be obedient instead of fleeing from God in rebellion?

There is much evidence to prove the existence of hell. If you don't believe those of us who have been there, then I urge you to read the Bible and do your own research on this subject. God gave you the freedom to choose either heaven or hell as your eternal destination. Please do not wait until it is too late to make a decision for Christ so that you can live eternally in His presence.

How do I make a decision for Christ and know that I will live eternally with Him when I die?

The first thing you must do is receive Jesus Christ as your Lord and Savior. Romans 10:9-10 says, "If you confess with your mouth the Lord Jesus and believe in your heart that God has raised Him from the dead, you will be saved. For with the heart one believes unto righteousness, and with the mouth confession is made unto salvation."

First John 1:9 says, "If we confess our sins, He is faithful and just to forgive us our sins and to cleanse us from all unrighteousness."

And Acts 3:19 tells us, "Repent therefore and be converted, that your sins may be blotted out, so that times of refreshing may come from the presence of the Lord."

In order to receive the free gift of salvation, you must believe, confess, and repent. When you have done that, God blots out all of your sins, as though they never existed. Here is a prayer of salvation and cleansing. If you sincerely pray this prayer, you have made a decision that you want to accept Christ and live eternally in His presence.

Heavenly Father, thank you for loving me so much that you sent your Son Jesus to die on a cross and carry my sins. I accept your free gift of salvation, and I ask you to forgive me of my sins and give me eternal life. Cleanse me of all my unrighteousness. Remove bitterness, unforgiveness, anger, strife, pride, greed, rejection, and rebellion from my life. I forgive and release those who have harmed me and wronged me. Cleanse me of everything I have been involved in that is ungodly in your sight. Break the strongholds of the enemy over my life. Break the power that I have given the enemy over my soul.

Help me to live righteously according to your word. I accept the victory and freedom that I now have in Christ Jesus. Help me to know your will for my life. Thank you for saving me and giving me eternal life. I pray this in Jesus' name. Amen.

The Bible also tells us that we should be baptized in water after we pray a prayer of salvation. Mark 16:16 says, "He who believes and is baptized will be saved." Please do not neglect this important step of water baptism.

Another important step in your decision is to begin to read the Bible. As a new believer, you might start with Matthew and read through the entire New Testament. Read at least a few chapters every day. Some people like to add chapters from Psalms and Proverbs to their daily reading. Then read the Old Testament, beginning with Genesis. Make a commitment to read through the entire Bible. When you have finished, read it again, because you will always discover things you missed the first time. The Bible is also available on CD for those who prefer listening over reading.

Spend time each day praising God and thanking Him for everything He has done and is doing in your life. Pray every day. I cannot stress enough the importance and the power of prayer. When I am alone with

God and on my knees in prayer, it is just God and me. There is no fear; nothing is brought up from my past.

Ask God to lead you to a powerful, Bible-believing church. Ask Him to help you live a life of holiness, not according to the rules of man, but according to His word. He wants to help you in your daily walk with Him; all you need to do is ask. When you sin, repent immediately. Don't let the enemy gain a foothold in your life. A few years ago, God told me to be consistent in my spiritual life. I could not start and then stop, start and then stop. That is excellent advice and I am glad to pass it on. I also told God that I knew witchcraft like the back of my hand, and I wanted to know more about Him than I did about the evil realm.

I pray that you will always remain faithful to Christ and that our Lord will bless you in your walk with Him. And if we do not meet on this side of heaven, we will meet some day on the other side.

CHAPTER 15

Scriptures for Personal or Group Study

"My people are destroyed for lack of knowledge."
- Hosea 4:6

In the following scripture references, how did Satan tempt Jesus? How did Jesus respond to the enemy after each attempt?

Matthew 4:1-11   Luke 4:1-13

What does the Bible tell us about temptation? Can temptation sometimes be a test to see how we will respond?

Genesis 3:1-5	Matthew 6:13	Ephesians 6:10-13
Psalm chapter 26	Matthew 18:6-7	James 1:12-15
Proverbs 1:10-19	Matthew 26:41	1 Peter 5:8-9
Proverbs 16:29	1 Corinthians 7:3-5	2 Peter 2:18-19
Proverbs 28:10	1 Corinthians 10:12-13	2 Peter 3:14-18
Ecclesiastes 7:26	Galatians 6:1	

How did Jesus deal with demonic spirits while He ministered on earth?

Mark 1:23-27	Luke 8:26-39	Luke 11:14-23
Luke 4:31-36	Matthew 9:32-34	Mark 1:32-34
Matthew 8:28-34	Matthew 12:22-30	Luke 4:40-41
Mark 5:1-20	Mark 3:20-30	

When Jesus called His twelve disciples, what power and authority did He give them? Do you believe that we have that same power and authority today?

Matthew 10:1   Mark 3:14-15   Matthew 10:7-8   Matthew 16:19

What does scripture say about anger?

Psalm 37:8	Proverbs 22:24	Ephesians 4:26-27 and 31
Proverbs 12:16	Proverbs 27:4	Colossians 3:8 and 21
Proverbs 14:17	Proverbs 29:22	Titus 1:7
Proverbs 15:1 and 18	Ecclesiastes 7:9	James 1:19-20
Proverbs 16:32	Amos 1:11	
Proverbs 19:11 and 19	Matthew 5:21-24	

How should we treat our enemies or those who have harmed or offended us?

Genesis 33:1-17	Proverbs 24:17-18	Acts 7:51-60
Genesis 45:1 -15	Proverbs 25:21-22	Romans 12:14
Genesis 50:15-22	Matthew 5:38-48	Romans 12:17-21
1 Samuel 24:1-22	Luke 6:27-36	1 Peter 3:8-9
Job 31:29-30	Luke 23:33-35	

What does scripture tell us about forgiveness toward those who have wronged us?

Matthew 6:12	Mark 11:25-26	Ephesians 4:32
Matthew 6:14-15	Luke 17:3-4	Colossians 3:12-15
Matthew 18:21-35	2 Corinthians 2:5-11	

What does the Bible tell us about obedience versus obstinacy and rebellion?

Deuteronomy 5:29-33	Proverbs 29:1	Romans 6:15-17
Deuteronomy chapter 6	Ecclesiastes 12:13-14	2 Corinthians
Deuteronomy 7:12-26	Isaiah 1:19-20	10:3-6
Deuteronomy chapters	Isaiah 48:18-19	Ephesians 5:6
8 and 9	Daniel 9:1-19	Hebrews 3:7-19
1 Samuel 12:13-25	Malachi 2:2	James 1:22-25
1 Samuel 15:22-26	Matthew 7:21-23	James 2:10-12
2 Chronicles 24:20	Luke 6:46-49	1 Peter 1:13-16
Psalm chapter 1	Luke 11:27-28	1 John 2:15-17
Psalm 107:10-21	John 9:31	1 John 4:20-21
Psalm 111:10	John 14:12-15 and 21-24	1 John 5:2-3
Psalm 112:1-10	John 15:1-14	
Proverbs 28:9 and 14	Acts 5:27-32	

What happens to a person when he repents and evil spirits leave him, yet he later turns his back on God and returns to a life of unrepentant sin? What does the Bible say about turning away from God?

Ezekiel 18:19-32	Galatians 4:9	Revelation 2:2-5
Matthew 12:43-45	1 Timothy 1:18-20	Revelation 2:19-23
Luke 11:24-26	Hebrews 10:26-31	Revelation 3:1-6
John 5:14	Hebrews 12:12-17	

Where did sin originate? What do we learn from these scriptures about Satan and his fallen angels?

Isaiah 14:12-15	Matthew 25:41	Mark 3:11	Luke 10:17-20
Ezekiel 28:15-17	Mark 1:23-27	Mark 5:7-13	John 8:44

1 Corinthians 10:20	2 Timothy 2:26	Genesis 3:1-15
2 Corinthians 4:3-4	1 Peter 5:8	Psalm 51:5
2 Corinthians 11:13-15	2 Peter 2:4	Psalm 58:3
Ephesians 6:12	James 2:19	Romans 5:12-14
Colossians 2:15	1 John 3:8	Revelation 12:7-10
2 Thessalonians 2:7-12	Jude verses 5-6	Revelation 16:12-14
1 Timothy 4:1	Genesis 2:16-17	Revelation 20:1-3

Sin has consequences. What are some of those consequences?

Genesis 3:16-24	Proverbs 6:12-15	Matthew 10:28
Exodus 20:5	Proverbs 10:27-29	Matthew 25:41-46
Exodus 32:33	Proverbs 11:19	Mark 3:28-30
Exodus 34:6-7	Proverbs 14:12	John 3:36
Leviticus chapter 26	Proverbs 28:9-10	John 5:28-29
Deuteronomy 31:16-18	Isaiah 3:9	John 8:34-36
Psalm 5:4-6	Jeremiah 12:17	Romans 2:4-9
Psalm 37:1	Jeremiah 15:13-14	Romans 6:23
Psalm 66:18	Lamentations 5:1-18	2 Thessalonians 1:8-9
Psalm 78:58-64	Daniel 12:2	1 John 2:11
Proverbs 1:22-32	Micah 3:4	Jude verses 4-11
Proverbs 3:33	Malachi 4:1	Revelation 21:8
Proverbs 5:22-23	Matthew 7:21-23	

What can you learn about hell and the final judgment from these verses?

Psalm 11:6	Proverbs 8:36	Matthew 7:21-23
Psalm 37:20	Ecclesiastes 12:13-14	Matthew 10:28
Psalm 55:15	Daniel 12:2-3	Matthew 12:31-37
Psalm 73:27	Malachi 4:1-3	Matthew 13:37-43 and 47-50
Psalm 140:10	Matthew 5:29-30	Matthew 23:29-33

Matthew 25:31-46	1 Corinthians 1:18-21	2 Peter chapter 2
Mark 16:16	1 Corinthians 6:9-10	2 Peter 3:3-9
Luke 13:3 and 23-28	Galatians 5:19-21	1 John 5:10-13
Luke 16:19-31	Ephesians 5:5	Jude verses 5-15
John 3:17-21	2 Thessalonians 1:6-9	Revelation 14:9-11
John 5:24-29	2 Thessalonians 2:9-12	Revelation 19:20
John 15:6	Hebrews 9:27-28	Revelation 20:4-5, 10-15
Romans 2:1-16	Hebrews 10:26-31	Revelation 21:8

Even Christians can open doors that will allow demonic spirits to influence or rule in their lives. To keep those doors closed, we must live a righteous and holy life, and repent when we fail. What is the warning to us in these scriptures?

Matthew 5:27-30	2 Corinthians 11:2-4	2 Timothy 4:3-4
Mark 7:15-23	2 Corinthians 12:20-21	Titus 1:15-16
John 3:17-20	Galatians 6:7-8	Hebrews 4:12-13
John 3:36	Ephesians 4:17-24	James 1:13-15
Romans 1:21-32	Ephesians 5:1-7	James 4:1-4
Romans 6:11-23	1 Timothy 4:1	1 Peter 4:1-6
Romans 8:1-11	2 Timothy 2:16-26	1 John 2:15-17
1 Corinthians 6:9-10	2 Timothy 3:1-9	Ezekiel 18:23-24

For what reasons might your prayers be hindered?

Deuteronomy 1:43-45	Isaiah 1:15-17	Matthew 6:7 and 14-15
Deuteronomy 3:26	Isaiah 59:1-8	Mark 11:25-26
2 Chronicles 15:2	Jeremiah 11:10-11	John 9:31
Psalm 66:18	Ezekiel 20:31	Hebrews 11:6
Proverbs 15:8	Daniel 10:10-14	James 1:6-8
Proverbs 21:13	Micah 3:4	James 4:2-10
Proverbs 28:9	Zechariah 7:12-13	1 Peter 3:7

What do these scriptures tell us about repentance, forgiveness of our sins, and living a righteous and holy life?

Matthew 4:17	1 Corinthians 5:9-13	Titus 2:1-15
Matthew 22:37-39	2 Corinthians 5:14-21	Titus 3:1-11
Mark 1:15	2 Corinthians 10:3-6	Hebrews 4:14-16
Mark 4:1-20	Galatians 3:22	Hebrews 12:1-17
Mark 7:20-23	Galatians 5:13-26	Book of James
John 3:1-21	Galatians 6:6-10	(5 chapters)
John 3:36	Ephesians 4:1-6	1 Peter chapter 4
John 8:31-36	and 17-32	1 Peter 5:5-11
John 10:27-28	Ephesians 5:1-14	2 Peter 1:5-11
John 13:34-35	Ephesians 6:10-18	1 John 1:5-10
John 14:12-15	Philippians 2:3-4 and 8	1 John 2:1-5
Acts 17:30	Colossians 1:9-23	and 15-17
Romans chapter 6	Colossians chapter 3	1 John 3:4-10
Romans 8:1-15	Colossians 4:1-8	and 16-18
Romans chapter 12	1 Thessalonians 5:12-22	1 John 4:17-21
Romans 14:10-13	1 Timothy 6:6-19	1 John 5:18-20
1 Corinthians 6:18-20	2 Timothy 2:16 and 22-26	

God has made many promises to those who repent and live righteous and holy lives. What do we learn about those promises and about heaven and eternal life in these scriptures?

Deuteronomy 7:9	Psalm 61:3	Psalm 107:8-9
Psalm 16:11	Psalm 62:1-2	Psalm 115:11, 13-14
Psalm chapter 23	Psalm 90:13-14	Proverbs 8:17
Psalm 33:18-22	Psalm chapter 91	Proverbs 8:34-35
Psalm 34:4-10 and 17-22	Psalm 94:18-19	Proverbs 9:10-11
Psalm 55:22	Psalm 103:2-19	Matthew 5:1-12

Matthew 6:19-21
and 25-34
Matthew 10:29-31
Matthew 25:34-36
John 3:14-17
John 9:31
John 10:9-11
John 10:28-29
John 11:25-26
John 12:46-47
John 14:1-6
John 14:12-18
John 14:25-27

John 15:7 and 11
John 16:33
Romans 5:8-11
Romans 6:22-23
Romans 8:26-28 and 31-39
1 Corinthians 2:9-10
1 Corinthians 15:20-26
1 Corinthians 15:51-57
2 Corinthians 4:16-18
2 Corinthians 7:6
Galatians 3:13-14
Ephesians 1:7
Ephesians 2:1-10

Ephesians 3:14-20
Philippians 4:13
and 19
Hebrews 11:6
Hebrews 13:5-6
James 1:12
James 2:5
1 Peter 1:3-9
1 Peter 5:6-7
Revelation 2:7, 11, 17
Revelation 3:5, 12, 21
Revelation chapters
21 and 22

pg 41
Darien, CT

pg 150
152
154
155
156
167

205
&
206

pg 121

190
191

Made in the USA
Middletown, DE
11 December 2016